THE PROPHET JONAH

A

THE PROPHET JONAH:
The Book and the Sign

BY

A. D. MARTIN

WITH AN INTRODUCTORY NOTE
BY
ARTHUR S. PEAKE, M.A, D.D.
Rylands Professor of Biblical Exegesis in
the University of Manchester

WIPF & STOCK · Eugene, Oregon

Wipf and Stock Publishers
199 W 8th Ave, Suite 3
Eugene, OR 97401

The Prophet Jonah
The Book and the Sign
By Martin, A. D. and Peake, Arthur S.
Softcover ISBN-13: 978-1-6667-3480-5
Hardcover ISBN-13: 978-1-6667-9107-5
eBook ISBN-13: 978-1-6667-9108-2
Publication date 9/7/2021
Previously published by Longmans, Green and Co., 1926

This edition is a scanned facsimile of
the original edition published in 1926.

If it may be permitted him in some sense to receive it—to know of it and haply to rejoice in its measure of Truth —this little book is given to

FREDERICK ARTHUR MARTIN,
2ND LIEUT. IN THE NOTTS. AND DERBY REGIMENT,

who fell at Ypres on September 7th, 1915.

NUNQUAM ANTEA QUAM HODIE CARIOR

CONTENTS

CHAPTER		PAGE
I.	AUTHOR'S PREFACE	1
II.	INTRODUCTORY NOTE BY DR. PEAKE	3
III.	TRANSLATION	7
	NOTE A: THE DIVINE NAME יהוה (Y H W H)	13
	NOTE B: THE POEM IN CHAPTER II	16
IV.	JONAH AS A FOLK-TALE	21
V.	THE PURPOSE AND CHARACTER OF THE BOOK	31
VI.	THE BOOK AS PROPAGANDA	49
VII.	THE ANATOMY OF BIGOTRY	57
VIII.	THE SIGN OF JONAH	69
IX.	THE SPIRIT OF CHRIST WHICH WAS IN THE AUTHOR	85
	NOTE C: THE LITERAL INTERPRETATION	99

I

AUTHOR'S PREFACE

THE purpose of these studies is to offer to the general reader an interpretation of the *Book of Jonah* in harmony with the best scholarship of our time. They do not, however, merely reproduce the opinions of others, but on several points offer suggestions arising out of an independent study of the Hebrew text

I have to express my most grateful thanks to Professor Peake, who not only has given me permission to utilise two articles which I contributed in 1921 and 1923 to the *Holborn Review*, so ably edited by him, but has also read my manuscript, helped me by his counsel upon some of the problems involved, and written an introductory note. My thanks are also due to his colleague, Professor W. L. Wardle, M A., D D , who has read my translation and made several comments thereon which I have been glad to adopt.

Messrs. Hodder & Stoughton have allowed me to republish (considerably enlarged) a paper on the *Sign of Jonah* which appeared in *The Expositor*, August, 1922, then under the editorship of the late Sir W. Robertson Nicoll. Mr. Humphrey Milford, of the Oxford University Press, also has kindly permitted me to make use of an article entitled, *Is a Christian Doctrine of Nationalism possible ?* which I wrote in 1921 for *The Constructive Quarterly*

A. D. M.

DANBURY,
   ESSEX.

II

INTRODUCTORY NOTE

AT the request of the author I contribute a brief Introduction to his book. Those who are familiar with his *Aspects of the Way* will need no other recommendation than this that the present book is by the same author. The earlier volume showed that on so long-studied and so well-worn a theme as the personality, the ministry and the work of Jesus he had fresh and beautiful things to say. And similarly he writes on the Book of Jonah in a manner worthy of the theme It is strange that some are so concerned to defend the literal historicity of the book and to make belief in it a touchstone of orthodoxy, that they fail to put the emphasis in the right place, their zeal for signs and wonders making them less sensitive than they might be to spiritual values. And there are others who are so obsessed by the portent that they profane by their ribald mockery the Holy of Holies For this book ranks with the greatest things the Old Testament has contributed to the literature of religion, with the autobiography of Hosea, with Jeremiah's prophecy of the New Covenant, with the close of the 73rd Psalm, with the fourth Servant poem (*Isa.* lii, 13—liii, 12) of which we commonly speak as the 53rd chapter of Isaiah. And it is justly ranked so high because it rises so nobly above all narrow patriotism and all religious bigotry in its vindication of God's universal grace and in its generous assurance of the willingness of the heathen to accept the truth and their readiness to heed the call to repentance.

That the book is the record of events in the life of Jonah, the prophet who predicted the splendid military successes of Jeroboam II, seems improbable in the last degree. And this not merely on account of the portents which it relates but because its whole attitude reflects a reaction under the influence of the Second Isaiah against the dominant tendencies of post-exilic Judaism. That an ancient legend forms the basis of the story is, I believe, unlikely; still more unlikely that Jonah actually went on a mission to Nineveh. The case for treating the story as an allegory in which Jonah stands for Israel and the episode of the fish for the exile and the restoration, is stronger than such interpreters as Sellin are willing to allow. But even if the book be regarded as pure fiction, it is fiction of the highest moral and religious value; and in its pregnant brevity, its vivid description, its narrative quality, its irony and its tenderness, a literary gem of the first water.

I have read Mr Martin's study with admiration and deep interest. I am impressed with the freshness of his observation, with the felicity of his expression, with the sympathetic realisation of the situation, with the power of imaginative reconstruction which he displays. The chapters on Jonah as a Folk-tale and The Sign of Jonah seem to me specially striking and suggestive. The searching dissection of bigotry and the application of Christian principles to our grave international problems deserve the most careful consideration. May he give us other books characterised by the same charm and distinction of style, the same gift of luminous exposition and keen analysis, the same power of probing the conscience and bracing the will.

ARTHUR S. PEAKE.

III

TRANSLATION

III

TRANSLATION

i, 1.   *Now the word of Yahweh[1] came to Jonah, the son of Amittai, saying,*
2.   *Rise up, go to Nineveh, the Great City, and denounce it; for their*
3.   *wickedness has affronted me. But Jonah rose up to get away to Tartessus from the presence of Yahweh: and he went down to Jaffa, and found a ship going to Tartessus: he paid his passage and went down into it to go with them to Tartessus from*
4.   *the presence of Yahweh. But Yahweh hurled a great wind upon the sea, so there was a great storm in the sea, and the ship reckoned herself*
5.   *doomed. Then the sailors were afraid, and every man cried to his particular god, and they hurled the ship's freightage into the sea, to abate its anger with them. But Jonah had gone into the vessel's innermost part,*
6.   *and was lying down fast asleep. And the Captain came to him and said, What do you mean by sleeping? get up and cry to your God; perhaps God will give a thought to us so that*

---

[1] See Note A on p. 13.

7. *we escape. And they said to one another, Come, let us cast lots that we may find out on whose account*
8. *this disaster is upon us. So they cast lots, and the lot fell upon Jonah. And they said unto him, Tell us please, on whose account this disaster has come upon us. What is your business ? And where do you come from ? What is your country, and*
9. *what is your nationality ? And he said unto them, A Hebrew am I, and it is Yahweh the God of Heaven whom I revere. He made both sea and land.*
10. *Then the men were terrified, and they said to him, What crime have you committed ? For the men knew that it was from the presence of Yahweh he was fleeing he had*
11. *confessed it to them. Then they said to him, What shall we do to you to calm the sea to us ? for the sea went*
12. *on raging. And he said to them, Lift me up and throw me to the sea, and the sea will be calm to you . for well I know that it is on my account this great storm is come upon you.*
13. *But the men rowed desperately to get the ship back to dry land However, they could not , for the sea went on*
14. *raging against them So they cried unto Yahweh and said, Ah ! now, we beseech Thee, Yahweh, let us not perish for taking this man's life, and lay not upon us innocent blood, for Thou Thyself, Yahweh, hast done as*
15. *it pleased Thee. So they lifted up*

THE BOOK AND THE SIGN

Jonah and threw him into the sea; and the anger of the sea subsided.

16. *Then the men had profound reverence for Yahweh, and offered sacrifices to Yahweh and made solemn vows.*

(Hebrew ii, 1)   17. *Now Yahweh appointed a great fish to swallow Jonah; and Jonah was in the belly of the fish three days and*

ii, 1. *three nights Then Jonah prayed unto Yahweh, his God, from the belly*

(,,   ii, 11)   ii, 10. *of the fish.*[1] *And Yahweh spoke to the fish and it vomited up Jonah on the dry land.*

(,,   ii, 3)   ii, 2. *And he (Jonah) said,*

I called from out my terrible straits unto Yahweh,
And He responded to me.
Out of the womb of Sheol I cried for help
Thou heardest my voice.

3. *For Thou hadst pitched me into ocean depths,*
the heart of the seas:
and the flood engulfed me.
All Thy breakers and Thy billows passed over me.

4. *And I—I thought, I am driven from Thy sight.*
How shall I ever look again toward Thy holy temple?

5. *Waters choked my breathing.*
The deep rolled round me.
Seaweeds were wound about my head.

6. *To the bases of the mountains I sank,*
To the land whose gates shut behind one for ever.

---

[1] See Note B on p. 16.

> *Yet Thou hast brought up my life*
> *from the pit,*
> *Yahweh my God*
> 7 *When my soul fainted within me I*
> *remembered Yahweh.*
> *And my prayer came in unto Thee—*
> *to Thy holy temple*
> 8. *They that observe vaporous vanities*
> *Forsake their own good God.*
> 9 *But as for me, with the music of*
> *thanksgiving*
> *I will sacrifice to Thee.*
> *What I have vowed I will perform.*
> *Salvation belongs to Yahweh.*

iii, 1. *And the word of Yahweh came to*
2. *Jonah the second time, saying, Up, go to Nineveh, the Great City, and proclaim against it the proclamation*
3. *which I will tell thee. And Jonah arose and went to Nineveh, in obedience to Yahweh's word. Now Nineveh was a city great even to God!*
4. *Three days' journey across! And Jonah penetrated the city a day's journey, and he shouted and said, When three[1] days are come and gone*
5. *Nineveh shall be overthrown! And the people of Nineveh believed in God, and they proclaimed a fast, and put on sackcloth from the greatest of them*
6. *even to the most insignificant. And the matter reached the king of Nineveh. He arose from his throne, and he took off his royal robe, and covered himself with sackcloth, and*

---

[1] The Greek version reads thus, not *forty days*. This is a more likely rendering.

THE BOOK AND THE SIGN

sat in ashes. And he had a proclamation made through Nineveh:

7. By order of the king and his nobles! Oyez! Man and beast, oxen and sheep shall not taste anything. They shall not feed. They shall not drink
8. water But let man and beast be covered with sackcloth, and let them cry vehemently to God. Let them turn every one from his evil way and from the violence
9. they are doing Who knows but that God may indeed turn and repent, and turn from His burning anger, so that we escape?
10. And God saw their doings that they turned from their evil way, and God repented of the evil which He said He would do to them, and He did it not.

iv, 1. But Jonah was very greatly displeased, and he blazed with anger
2. about it. And he prayed to Yahweh and said, Ah! Yahweh, was not this what I said when I was yet in my own land? Why, it was because of this I tried to forestall Thee by fleeing to Tartessus, for I knew that Thou art a gracious and pitying God, slow to anger, and of large love, and repentant
3. of evil Now then, Yahweh, pray take my life from me, since for me
4. death is better than life. And Yahweh said, Are you very angry?[1]
5. Then Jonah went out of the city, and

---

[1] The Hebrew having two possible renderings here, I follow the one which agrees with the Greek version.

sat on its eastward side, and made for
himself there a booth, and sat under
it in the shade, until he should see
6. what might happen in the city. And
the God Yahweh ordained that a
gourd should come up above Jonah to
be a shadow over his head to deliver
him from his evil case And Jonah
was very happy indeed about the
7. gourd. But, the next day, in the
lifting of the morning dusk, God
appointed a worm to attack the gourd,
8. and it withered. And it fell out that
when the sun rose God appointed a
sultry east wind, and it attacked
Jonah's head, so that he swooned.
Then he asked for himself that he
might die. For me, he said, death is
9. better than life And God said to
Jonah, Are you so very angry about
the gourd ? And he said, I am very
angry about it · I could die with
10. anger ! Then Yahweh said, You
have had a love for the gourd, which
you have not laboured at, or made to
grow. Child of a night it sprang up,
and child of a night it perished.
11. And I—should not I have pity upon
Nineveh, the Great City, which has
in it more than twelve times ten
thousand persons, who do not know
how to distinguish their right hand
from their left, and also much cattle ?

NOTE A

THE DIVINE NAME יהוה (Y H W H)

THE English Revisers of the Old Testament state in their preface that following the practice of the Authorised Version they have substituted for " the ineffable Name," which they call JEHOVAH, the title LORD or GOD (printed in small capitals) There are objections, however, to such a procedure. LORD is too general to be a true equivalent for a personal name, and GOD is not much less inadequate. As S. Paul wrote, *There are gods many and lords many* (*I Cor.* viii, 5). All the distinctiveness of the proper name of the God of Israel is lost if we are content with such general terms. Moreover, LORD, as S. Paul further remarks, is a title which Christians associate with Jesus Christ. To apply one and the same title to the Being whom the Hebrews regarded as their national deity, to whom also, in certain epochs of their long history they did not hesitate to ascribe some of the most appalling decrees ever enunciated by any religion, and to Him who came as the Representative of the Father and as the Messenger of universal goodwill, is to telescope the several stages of Revelation into that confusion of thought which is the prolific cause of scepticism.

There are objections also to the word JEHOVAH. Most readers are aware that the four letters which constitute the whole of the name in Hebrew are all consonants ; the Hebrew people having ever been accustomed to write their language without vowels and to insert the latter, when required in public reading, according to an oral tradition.

Now the objection which philologists take to JEHOVAH is that it is a hybrid, the vowels selected in order to pronounce the name being those that belong properly to a totally different collection of consonants. The objection is a technical one but it should be respected. It must be confessed, too, that the word thus queerly formed is not beautiful, and such currency as it has had among Christians has mostly been in association with somewhat narrow types of piety.

It is impossible to discuss this matter, even in a brief note, without alluding to the rendering adopted by Dr. Moffatt in his very valuable *New Translation*. With evident hesitation this famous scholar has rendered Y H W H by THE ETERNAL. The sonorous, almost onomatopœic quality of the rendering suits wonderfully well in such a passage as the 23rd *Psalm—The Eternal shepherds me, I lack for nothing*[1]—but one stumbles at this in *Exodus* xxxii, 14, *So the Eternal changed his mind*[1] If the idea of an eternal existence really belongs to the word—and this is still a matter in dispute—it certainly cannot have been operative in the bulk of the passages where it is found. The truth is that the habits of religious people in speaking of the deities they revere are not dissimilar from those they and all others follow in speaking of their fellow men. Even with a knowledge of Greek, one does not necessarily think of the interests of husbandry when speaking of king GEORGE (Greek, *georgos*, a husbandman), although sometimes we may remember that he exhibits at agricultural shows In the same way an ancient Divine name is, in common usage, a means of identifying a person believed actually to exist, and in the case before us of naming One who was ever overshadowing men's previous experience of Him with new revelations of His character.

In view of all the uncertainty which still attaches to the origin and purpose of the Name, I have ventured in this little book to adopt the form which scholars generally

[1] Moffatt.

THE BOOK AND THE SIGN

approve, that given in the *Oxford Lexicon*, and in *Peake's Commentary*, and which Dr. Moffat in the preface to his translation agrees is correct—YAHWEH (pronounced Yah-way, the first *h* having its full guttural force, with almost but not quite the sound of *ch* as in the Scots word *loch*). Because this is the true form of the word we should surely try to give it currency. And it has a beauty of its own, which is no small consideration ; for the value of a name lies not merely in its appellative convenience, nor simply in any meaning it may possibly register, but also in the kind of sound with which it is spoken. There is a suggestion of the indeterminate in the first syllable YAH—which for ourselves invests the whole word with significance, and may sometimes remind us, that whatever harshness belonged to certain phases of Old Testament religion, there was always an outlooking from it towards the Infinite and a view of the processional quality of life.

NOTE B

THE POEM IN CHAPTER II

AS the Hebrew text stands the poem contained in chapter ii is the prayer of Jonah offered from within the belly of the fish An examination of the poem, however, reveals the fact that it is a delightfully embellished thanksgiving for a deliverance actually experienced. Some eminent critics have suggested that there is no inconsistency here. They regard the great fish as the actual instrument of Jonah's escape from death. That is difficult. If one were dealing with the element opposite to water, one would be inclined rather to quote the homely proverb, "Out of the frying-pan into the fire." For there are indications in the Old Testament that the fear and dislike of the sea entertained by the Hebrew people, though due in part to mere unfamiliarity with its infinitely varying moods, was caused also by belief in the existence of the creatures that lived in its depths. There was the chaos-monster, Rahab, ever insurgent against the Divine Being [1] There were other monsters and great fish more tractable and yet terrifying to the imagination. One of these was hardly likely to be conceived of as an angel of deliverance for a drowning man. Further, as we shall find when we come to discuss the purpose of the *Book of Jonah*, the symbolic meaning of the great fish and its swallowing of the prophet set forth not deliverance, but an undoubted calamity in Israel's life [2] I conclude, therefore, that the intention of the author was rather to suggest that Yahweh had now safely trapped his

[1] *Job* xxvi, 12. *Isaiah* li, 9, etc
[2] See p. 33, and Dr. Peake's Introductory Note.

THE BOOK AND THE SIGN 17

erring servant, and held him at last at His sovereign disposal In such circumstances language of thanksgiving could hardly be expected from Jonah. For this reason, and also because the poem describes an escape from drowning rather than from a sea-monster's maw many modern scholars treat it as an interpolation by another hand.[1] I have not felt it necessary, however, to take this view. In the first place, is it not highly probable that the author would feel bound to place some lyrical outburst of thanksgiving upon the prophet's lips when actually *terra firma* was reached, as in the case of Hezekiah's deliverance from mortal sickness (*Isaiah* xxxviii) ? And the extremely beautiful piety of the poem, its wistful outlooking towards God, its humble thankfulness help to build up the climax of the story by shewing how, even after not only deliverance from death but spiritual renewal, old blind prejudices may still persist and reassert their sway, just as Hezekiah's psalm of thanksgiving is followed immediately by a lapse into worldly pride [2] Again, when we come later to the interpretation of Jonah in terms of national history we shall see the counterpart of all this in Israel's life.

It is of course true that Jonah's psalm does not reflect very clearly Jonah's terrible situation within the fish. To have made it do this would have involved a disgusting piece of realism such as one may read in that fourteenth century alliterative version of *Jonah* entitled *Patience*, recently reissued by Sir Israel Gollancz. One turns back from this English paraphrase to the Hebrew original with a new sense of the latter's charm and delicacy of touch. I believe the Hebrew writer deliberately allowed his imagination to escape a little from the framework of his narrative, in order to make the suggestion of mortal peril as powerful as possible without involving nauseous particulars.

At the same time, as already indicated, there is an un-

[1] See *Peake's Commentary in loc.* and the *International Critical Commentary.*
[2] *Isaiah* xxxix.

doubted difficulty in representing the prayer of a man swallowed by a sea-monster as a grateful retrospect of a trouble passed away A triumphant faith such as that inculcated by our Lord, *All things whatsoever ye pray and ask for, believe that ye have received them, and ye shall have them*,[1] is hardly to be looked for in the Old Testament, nor would it be germane to the somewhat artistic character of the psalm.

We notice, however, that the poem refers back (English version II, 7) to a previous prayer offered while the prophet lay in a fainting condition It is possible to regard this fainting prayer as that sent up from out the fish's belly, and by the slight rearrangement of the order of the verses made in the translation, to read the hymn of chapter ii as spoken after Jonah reached dry land. This is the position adopted by some modern scholars and the one which appeals most to my own judgement.

[1] *S Mark* xi, 24

IV

JONAH AS A FOLK-TALE

Jewish folk-lore contains a large number of legends setting forth the relations of man with his Maker The character of many of these legends has been indicated by Dr Immanuel Olšvanger in his recent essay CONTENTIONS WITH GOD *(Hasefer Agency for Literature, London) Quaint, expostulatory, daring, they disclose the common mind of Israel in many ages, many lands, as freely drawing upon the imagination for the elucidation of righteousness. They show us how naturally such a story as Jonah would circulate orally, apart from any currency it might have in manuscript, and how the common people of Israel would delight the more readily in Jonah's quarrel with his God, because thereby the Divine goodness was the more wonderfully revealed In this section, accordingly, the writer has attempted by the aid of imagination to reproduce the primitive oral circulation of the story of Jonah*

IV

JONAH AS A FOLK-TALE

ON an evening more than 2,000 years ago—it needs not now to say how many more—a few shepherds in the wilderness of Horeb pitched their black worsted tents near a trickle of water that escaped from the mountain's side. They made ready their supper of camel-milk, boiling it over a dung-fire, and baked oil-cake thereat, and unpacked a handful of dates and some salt. The sun fell swiftly. Stars broke through the purplish-blue heaven. In the distance wild creatures howled from fear or hunger. The tent's warm protection was welcome for scantily clad men, and as they sat beside a single dim lamp, after far-separated labours and long silence, one told to another his tale of the day's simple adventures—the sight of a strayed cormorant come up from distant sea-rocks, a basilisk lurking amid the burning sands, dust of a far-off caravan crawling from Egypt, and last, the counting of the sheep as they passed down to the water and—thanks to the Almighty—not one missing

This night more yet was to be said. For of a sudden came a stirring among the tethered camels. A dog barked furiously. Herdsmen hastened in with news of a traveller dimly discernible fifty yards away, crying out to them that he might tarry for a night.

They brought him in and set salt and cakes before him and such milk as was left; and he, exhausted by long searching for some track obliterated by sudden siroccos, ate and drank, giving God thanks. Thereafter they questioned him of his name and country and of the great world of cities they so seldom entered. Calling himself Ben-Ammi (the Son of my people), the stranger answered their questions, and then told of one whom he had met upon the road from Hebron, a learned man, who had offered him a scripture, saying, ' Read this, I pray thee,' but he had perforce answered, ' I cannot for I am not learned ' Whereat the stranger had sat down beside him under a juniper tree and had read to him the book, telling him many words besides that explained the book, all which, because the story he related was most wondrously full of the Spirit of God, he could remember to speak again.

The story was this. There dwelt in Galilee a prophet of Yahweh named Jonah. Often had this man of God seen from the hill-tops of his country great armies of the Gentiles, with their hot-breathed horses, and with a multitude of chariots whose wheels glittered in the sun like bundles of swords. And, because he loved peace and ease and contemplation, the heart of Jonah was wrathful at the frequency of battles and at the laying waste of the cornfields and vineyards He hated the very name of the Assyrian. His own people of Israel he esteemed as God's elect son. Also, being a Hebrew of the Hebrews, he held to the ancient ways of worship, and loved to ponder the words of the prophets before him. To his neighbours he often spoke of the greatness of Yahweh, pointing to the stars and asking, *Who hath created these that bringeth out their host by number ?* And often he would sing the words of the son of Jesse, *I love thee, O Yahweh, my Strength.* But with the passing of time there worked a change in him. For although Jonah saw and heard enough of the armies of the heathen that came and went, yet, his home being hidden away amongst the hills, he himself dwelt securely, and had nought to trouble him. Indeed, full of ease, the spirit in the prophet began to slumber, and he ceased at last to speak the word of Yahweh to the people. No disciples gathered about him to write down and treasure his oracles. And the placid years came, wherein a man

THE BOOK AND THE SIGN 23

ceases to see the visions of youth and dreams not as yet the dreams of old men. He spent these mid years of life as a tale that is told.

But it came to pass, on a day when Jonah sat under his figtree, watching the flying of a hoopoe that nested near by, a youth came running to him and spake of the Assyrians, how they had smitten down the people that dwelt by Megiddo, slaying the men with the sword, and carrying away their wives and daughters to Nineveh Jonah stirred himself a little and muttered in reply, ' It is Yahweh, let Him do what seemeth Him good.' ' Nay, father Jonah,' said the youth, ' but Yahweh surely hath need of one to rebuke the enemy and the devourer of His people.' And he departed from him.

Thereafter Jonah slept, and in his dream he saw, and lo ! a mighty city, with walls high and lifted up against heaven, thronged with a strange people. Over the city in a dark sky was the flame of a sword held by burning seraphim Vast was its sweep, tearing the black clouds. And Jonah awoke hearing a voice that said, Arise, go to Nineveh, the Great City, and shout against it , for their wickedness affronts me.

In the sweat of his brow he girt his loins, and took a staff in his hand, and put bread and wine and silver in his scrip, and set out upon his journey. But even as he went, another voice spake within him bidding him stay beside the pleasant vineyards of Gath-Hepher. Why should he thrust himself into a lion's den ? What avail was it to speak of justice and judgement to the heathen ? Let Yahweh pour out His wrath upon them, and that suddenly as when a robber slays, and then strips the slain, at midnight. So Jonah thought within himself and counted the word of Yahweh a foolish thing, and despised the counsel of the Almighty.

Yet did he not dare to turn back, lest all his neighbours who had seen him depart should mock at his return. Moreover the hand of Yahweh was upon him ; there was, as it were, a burning fire shut up in his bones. He thought to find no relief save in leaving Yahweh's land for some far-off Western shore. So he turned to the South and came down to Joppa, a city of the uncircumcised Philistines, and there he found a ship about to sail for Tartessus, in the land of the sunset beyond the Great Sea. And he paid the fare for this long journey, for he was a rich man and had lived in plenty. Then as one afraid he hastened down into the lowest part of the ship, and hid himself amongst the bales of Tyrian cloths and coils of hempen rope. Now also as the ship rode upon the waves the vision of the word of Yahweh ceased from Jonah's heart. He was free, for was he not escaped from Yahweh's land? But still in his memory fell echoes of words he had spoken to the people in days long past, wherein he had declared that Yahweh was Lord of heaven and earth and sea. Wearied out with his journey and angry and hopeless, at last he slept deeply.

Now, continued Ben-Ammi, when the Scribe told me the story thus far I trembled, for I bethought me of Jordan when it overfloweth its banks, and of Chinnereth on the way to Damascus, and of the sea of the Arabah whose waters are bitter, and all these are often troubled with tempest yet ever have the land about them. But the Great Sea stretcheth to the sky and no man knoweth the end thereof. Thou shudderest, said the learned man, and truly the power of Yahweh is not shortened to the hills and rocks and the cities of Israel. He blew His breath upon the sea. The ship's sails were torn to pieces and she crouched between the waves, as a woman with flying hair crouches in terror, fearing a breaking blow. And on the ship every mariner was crying to his god But there was no god that heard. Then because the waves were snapping the tacklings, the shipmaster and the mariners went down into the hold to take up their wares and to cast them into the sea And amongst them lo! Jonah asleep What! cried the shipmaster bitterly, will sleeping help us? Arise and call upon thy God, if perchance God will give thought to our plight and rescue us.

THE BOOK AND THE SIGN 25

Then also one of the seamen said to his fellows, Come and let us cast lots that we may see who of us is the cause of this disaster. The lot fell upon Jonah ! Then they questioned him and he told them how he feared Yahweh who had made both the sea and the dry land. And because he saw that the face of Yahweh was against him, he bade them cast him as a prey to the roaring sea. But the men, though they were of the Gentiles, and knew not Yahweh, were kindly, and they plunged their oars into the sea, rowing hard to get back to Joppa Howbeit the sea grew more and more angry. Then did they pray to the God of Jonah to be merciful unto them, and if they did unto His servant as he had requested, not to charge them with shedding innocent blood. When, therefore, they had prayed, two of them lifted up the prophet and threw him into the raging waves ; wide open and dark were his eyes amid the white crested waters , then he sank out of their sight. At once the wind ceased and the waves gnashed upon the ship no more Then the mariners were filled with fear, and they hastened and offered unto Yahweh a sacrifice of young pigeons which, after the manner of the Gentiles, they had taken with them for the discernment of omens. And they made vows and worshipped Yahweh.

Now Yahweh had created the great sea-monsters, and he ordered one of these to swallow Jonah. Then was Jonah three days and three nights in the monster's belly And his soul fainted within him, and he prayed to Yahweh from the bottom of the deep sea, amid the rocky roots of the mountains, where, amongst the weeds, the monster had his home. And his prayer came up through the green waters, and like a white sea-bird that rises crying to its mate in the high cleft above the breaking billows it entered into the temple of Yahweh in heaven. So Yahweh bade the sea-monster to cast Jonah out upon the dry land. And the sea-monster did so. Then did Jonah sacrifice unto Yahweh with the voice of thanksgiving.

As he was worshipping, lo ! the word of Yahweh came to

him a second time saying, Arise, go unto Nineveh, the Great City, and proclaim against it the proclamation that I bid thee. So Jonah went to Nineveh. Now Nineveh was a city, great even in the sight of God. Three days were needed for a man to travel from one end of it to the other. And Jonah journeyed in it one whole day, saying nought to any man. But on the second day he began to preach, and he said, In three days' time Nineveh shall be overthrown. And the people of Nineveh believed God's word. Even the king of Nineveh heard about Jonah, and he left his throne, and cast aside his robe, and girt himself with sackcloth, sitting down amid ashes. Also he commanded the people everywhere to fast, neither to eat nor drink, nor to give to their cattle, but all to wear sackcloth, even the beasts in the fields and the oxen in the stalls. Let all, he said, turn away from evil and from violence and pray to God, if so be God will have mercy upon us. Then did God repent of the evil He had said He would do unto them, and He did it not.

Now Jonah went on his way through the city still preaching and saying, Nineveh shall be destroyed in three days. And everywhere the heralds of the king followed, making proclamation that men should mourn and fast and turn from their evil ways. And it was as when reapers with their sickles cut down the thick-standing corn in the field: as they went through the city, the people, hearing the word of Yahweh and of the king prostrated themselves upon the ground with weeping and crying and mourning. And lo! the third day came and Jonah looking back saw and heard the lamentation of the people. And he was very angry indeed because they repented, for he knew that in their repentance they would be forgiven. So he prayed that Yahweh would take away his life from him. But Yahweh only said unto him, Art thou very angry?

Jonah answered not again to Yahweh, but went out of the city. In his anger he tore down some branches of a tree and made himself a booth and sat in its shadow watch-

THE BOOK AND THE SIGN

ing the city, if so be that even yet Yahweh would destroy it. But there came no storm-cloud in the sky, neither was there any shaking of the earth.

Now the leaves of the branches Jonah had cut for his booth soon withered in the sun, and so God caused a gourd to spring up beside it that the broad green leaves of the gourd might make a shade for Jonah, just as men often plant the gourd beside a lodge in a garden of cucumbers to grow upon the poles thereof. So Jonah rejoiced greatly in the gourd. But God sent a worm next day to smite the gourd, and all its pleasant leafage withered away. Also God sent the sirocco, blowing very softly, and in the heat of the sun Jonah's spirit fainted within him, and again he asked God that he might die

Then did God answer him, Art thou very angry about the gourd? And Jonah said, Very angry I am; I could die with anger And Yahweh said, Thou hast cared for the gourd, although thou hast not laboured over it, neither madest it to grow, the offspring of the night-dews, perishing too in a night. Should not I have pity upon the people of Nineveh, the work of my own hands, a multitude whom I have fed and nourished from their childhood, more than six score thousand of them, all ignorant of the way they should walk in? And should I not pity also their innocent cattle?

Through the tent-door came the peaceful light of the jewelled sky. Ben-Ammi rose and led the shepherds forth, saying, Look now toward Heaven. Wide are the ways of the Almighty, and many are the stars. So likewise is His mercy upon His servant Ben-Ammi, and upon every son of every people, and upon every living thing which God hath created and made.

V

THE PURPOSE AND CHARACTER OF THE BOOK

[*Throughout this and the succeeding studies I distinguish the Scripture from the prophet by naming the former the* BOOK OF JONAH, *as in the English versions one reads the* BOOK OF ESTHER, *and the* BOOK OF JOB, *etc*]

V

THE PURPOSE AND CHARACTER OF THE BOOK

ANY satisfactory exposition of this Scripture must deal with the things in the book itself, unencumbered by references to it elsewhere Thus our Lord's allusions to Jonah, which will be discussed in a later chapter, do not here concern us at all It may, however, be said at once that such references as He made have little or nothing in common with the main purpose of the book. Whereas Jesus was thinking of the impact of Jonah upon the Ninevites, the author evidently desired to exhibit the character of Jonah in respect to the Divine mercy upon Nineveh It is clear that Jesus only used the book for the purposes of an illustration. At the same time, since He referred to the Ninevites as standing up at the Last Judgement with the men of His own generation, it is also clear that He treated the book as historical He would do this simply because of its narrative form Had the question of its historicity been raised in His time, and been viewed in the lights with which for us it is invested, it is possible His usage of the book might have been accompanied by some qualification safeguarding its true literary character. Certainly He, whose favourite teaching-method was the parable, a method evidently selected for the quickening of thought in individual minds, would have been no party to any closuring of free enquiry, nor to the introduction in the discussion of any merely arbitrary authority.[1] As loyal Christian disciples, therefore, we are free to examine our subject in its proper place as a book of the Old Testament having its occasion and

[1] See further the Note C, on page 99, at the end of the book.

meaning long before Jesus spoke. Similar to His use of the Scripture—broad, general, untechnical—would be that first oral circulation of the story it told, which has been suggested in the previous section. Looking at it more closely, however, we can see it had a mission particular to the author's time That mission is now our concern.

In the enquiry before us, we shall find that the allegorical interpretation is the only method of reading the *Book of Jonah* which can do full justice to its artistic quality. The more closely it is studied the more sure we are that the writer has freely quarried in the realms of both Nature and the Supernatural for the purpose of expressing one paramount truth.

Now if the story is an allegory, it is unnecessary to suppose that a prophet named Jonah ever visited Nineveh at all. Symbolic journeys and actions were sometimes made by the Hebrew prophets, but it would appear that at other times they were content, after having publicly announced them, to take such things as done Thus, Ezekiel was commanded to lie down upon his couch, first of all on his left side for a period of 390 days, and then on his right side for 40 days, all the time being bound with cords, that he might represent to the people God's judgement upon the sins of Israel and of Judah respectively (*Ezekiel* iv, 4-8).[1] Did he really lie in bed so uncomfortably for some thirteen months in order to illustrate the impending punishment of his nation's sins ? Similarly Jeremiah was bidden to make two journeys to the River Euphrates[2] in order that by first burying his girdle there, and then later on recovering it he might effectively picture to the people of Jerusalem Yahweh's power to mar their pride (*Jeremiah* xiii, 1-4). We can hardly think he really went , and in view of all the circumstances involved, the journey of Jonah to Nineveh

[1] The actual numbers should perhaps be read differently. This, however, is immaterial

[2] It is possible, though not probable, that Parah near Anathoth, rather than Euphrates, is intended This would lessen but not destroy the force of my illustration.

THE BOOK AND THE SIGN 33

and his preaching there in a foreign language, is almost equally improbable. Indeed, for the purposes of the author of the *Book of Jonah*, it is not essential, at most only a happy subsidiary fact, that any prophet of this name actually existed at all Pure works of fiction, however, are not so much to be looked for in Hebrew literature as imaginative and free reconstructions of actual events, and it is possible the story of Jonah starts from an historic basis. All that now we can discern of that foundation is the fact that a prophet of this name is referred to in *II Kings* xiv, 25, as having foretold an extension of the kingdom of Israel under Jeroboam II. We shall consider later such significance as he possesses for this book that bears his name.

The foundation of the allegory of Jonah lies in *Jeremiah* li, 34-44 Israel is heard bitterly complaining: *Nebuchadrezzar the King of Babylon hath devoured me, he hath set me as an empty vessel, he has swallowed me up like a monster, he hath filled his maw with my delicacies ; he hath rinsed me out* ' *The violence done to me and my flesh be upon Babylon !* ' *let the inhabitants of Zion say ; and* ' *My blood be upon the inhabitants of Chaldæa !* ' *let Jerusalem say. Therefore thus saith Yahweh · Behold, I will defend thy cause and take vengeance for thee. . . . And I will punish Bel in Babylon, and I will bring forth out of his mouth that which he hath swallowed up : and the nations shall not flow together any more unto him · yea, the wall of Babylon is fallen !*[1] Here we have a pictorial representation of the Exile and the Return under the figure of the swallowing of a man by a sea-monster and his subsequent ejectment from the monster's mouth. In the same way Jonah's adventure in the sea figuratively expresses the Captivity and the Return, the prophet first of all representing his nation and then more particularly the whole order of the prophets in his time.

Before looking at this any further a glance at certain

[1] Driver's translation.

other features of the story will make clear the high improbability of any literal interpretation. Consider the penitence of the Ninevites, not its suddenness and completeness but the grotesque form it takes. The decree of the king and his nobles requires ·a universal abstinence from food and water not only by the people but also by their numerous flocks and herds. Both men and beasts are to be clothed in sackcloth and—if we are really to be literal—all together to cry vehemently to God for His mercy Conceive the picture and listen to the petitions and bellowings of this vast and mixed assembly ! Conservative commentators have diligently sought out from Herodotus and other ancient writers (e g , *Judith* iv, 9-15) stories of domestic animals that were made to bear the trappings of mourning, as until recently was the case with our own funeral horses , but I find no instance of cattle being called upon to participate in the prayers of their masters, although, no doubt, they might somehow vocalise their distress The thing is preposterous if the narrative is history it is exquisite if it is the irony of fiction [1] Had we met with the king of Nineveh's decree in the pages of *Sir John Mandeville* we should scarcely have failed to recognise its lurking humour, a quality which peeps out again in Yahweh's question to His sulky servant, *Are you very angry ?* as also in the words about the shadow of the miraculously growing gourd being granted the prophet *to deliver him from his evil case.*

But the particular literary quality of the book reaches its fullest expression in the expostulation of Jonah when Nineveh is spared He is displeased, and his displeasure has been explained by some as occasioned by the apparent stultification of his prediction. Hebrew prophecy, however, was always contingent At least five times in the Old Testament God is said to have repented of the evil He had threatened. Jeremiah formally laid down what we

[1] Taking the latter view I find it unnecessary to suppose, with some scholars, an error here in the Hebrew text.

THE BOOK AND THE SIGN 35

may call the doctrine of the Divine Mobility—God's freedom to change His mind, as man changes his—in the following passage : *The word of Yahweh came to me saying . . . At what instant I shall speak concerning a nation, and concerning a kingdom, to pluck up and to break down and to destroy it ; if that nation concerning which I have spoken, turn from their evil, I will repent of the evil that I thought to do unto them* [1] So Jonah's menace to the Ninevites must in his own mind have depended for its fulfilment upon their continuance in sin. And, indeed, this is implied in his remonstrance to Yahweh. Before he set out on his journey, he declares, he knew what the issue of his preaching would be, namely that they would be forgiven. He has even the audacity to say that he had hoped by fleeing to Tartessus to forestall and thwart the gracious purpose of the message which he was commissioned to take. Apparently in his tremendous egotism he has forgotten that he is not the only messenger at Yahweh's command Surely the frame of mind revealed in his language here is a very curious one for a prophet of Yahweh, so curious in fact as inevitably to raise the question, Would any real Hebrew prophet ever speak like this ? Can such a misanthropic man have been a living prophet at all ? *Ah ! Yahweh, was not this what I said when I was yet in my own land ? Why, it was because of this I tried to forestall Thee by fleeing to Tartessus for I knew*[2] *that thou art a gracious God, slow to anger, and plenteous in mercy, and repentest thee of the evil.* Is this, indeed, a possible prayer ? We notice that the phrases employed about Yahweh are just the current watchwords of Israel's piety Most of them meet us over and over again in the Old Testament. Taken together they have here the force of a creed and appear to be borrowed direct from *Joel* ii, 13. Yahweh *is gracious, and full*

---

[1] For the full doctrine see the whole passage *Jeremiah* xviii, 1-10, and compare also *Ezekiel* xviii, 20ff

[2] I quote the rest of the prayer from the Revised Version, in order that the reader may the more easily recognise the conventionality of Jonah's description of his God.

of compassion, slow to anger, and plenteous in mercy, and repenteth him of the evil. Now to make Jonah ascribe these beautiful qualities to his God as the reason for refusing to preach about Him is excellent irony but impossible history. No Hebrew prophet would have dared to use in prayer to Yahweh the most classic words on the Divine mercy to be found in the speech of his countrymen, as a reason for disapproving the exercise of that mercy. It would be almost as though an English Christian prayed to his Lord, ' I knew that Thou camest into the world to save sinners and therefore when Thou calledst me to preach Thy Gospel in India I fled to New York.' Our actions and negligences may be as inconsistent with creed as this, but we do not commonly flaunt them in the face of God with quite such open cynicism The *Book of Jonah* seems clearly revealed here as a piece of vigorous and yet delicate satire, and its hero to be as truly a literary creation as, say, Sir Hudibras or Don Quixote

It will help us to see the cogency of the appeal of the book if we can place it in relation to Hebrew history. There is general agreement that it was written after the Exile, yet not later than the third century, B C. Various dates between 400 and 200 B C have been assigned for its composition. Dr. Bewer, in the *International Critical Commentary*, leaves the matter undetermined between these limits. Dr. Peake, in his *Commentary*, places it in the fourth or the third century. Sir George Adam Smith, in the *Expositor's Bible*, appears to favour a time somewhere about the year 300, say 130 years after the work of Ezra and Nehemiah. If we may choose a fairly early date and bring the book into relation with the restored community, while those religious forces which Ezra and Nehemiah represented were in full operation, we shall obtain a most relevant situation.

The attitude of post-exilic Israel to the outside world always appears to our minds a lamentable declension from the lofty teaching of *Isaiah* xl-lv. The impressive feature

THE BOOK AND THE SIGN 37

of that great work of prophecy, written mostly on the eve of the Return, is its universal outlook and its missionary appeal. Israel, as the servant of Yahweh, is to be a light to the Gentiles. We read the splendid oracles contained in *Isaiah* xlii, xliii, xlix, lii, 13—liii, lv, and then turn to the records of the restored community in Jerusalem, with its anti-Samaritan feuds, and polemic against those mixed marriages the *Book of Ruth* seems to have been written to justify, and we wonder that so great a voice should have awakened echoes so few in men who were unquestionably devout. Amongst the acknowledged writers of the time and of the century immediately following we see no one upon whom the mantle of the great prophet of the Exile, the Second Isaiah, had evidently fallen. On the contrary the author of *Zechariah* ix-xiv, a Scripture probably later than the *Book of Jonah*, confessed to the existence of very unworthy elements in the men of his order As a moral force prophetism was surely spent, was, indeed, bankrupt, when it could be said by Yahweh of a time of coming blessing, *I will cause the prophets and the unclean spirit to pass out of the land*, and when this could be supported by a picture of the prophet as a dervish-fanatic with self-inflicted wounds, shamefacedly disowning his own frenzy (*Zechariah* xiii, 2-6).

At some time, then, in these epochs of religious narrowness and atavistic prophetism, the *Book of Jonah* was written, not as a work of prophecy, but, in the first place, as a satire upon the contemporary prophetic order, and, in the second place, as an arraignment of the nation whom the prophets represented. It is probably the work of one whom we should call a layman, a man of literary culture and of outlook broadened by travel, with a heart whose affluence included humour and sympathy as far-reaching as that of any mind in the Old Testament.

I have ventured to compare his portraiture of Jonah with Butler's *Sir Hudibras* or with the *Don Quixote* of Cervantes. For various reasons the latter comparison is the pleasanter and the more suitable It may be worth while in a few sentences to establish this reference.

Although, of course, in bulk there is a great difference between these two masterpieces in the literature of satire, yet if the Spanish work through its quantity has a cumulative effect to which the Hebrew story can make no claim, we may yet say of the latter ·

> In small proportions we just beauties see ;
> And in short measures life may perfect be.

Both works had a serious moral purpose. Prescott, in his essay on Cervantes, reviewing the intellectual and moral temper of Spain in the sixteenth century, draws attention to the mischievous influence exerted by the books of chivalry then so widely current. The mind of the Spanish people was debauched and their morals were impaired by foolish and impossible stories of knight-errantry. So much was this the case that in 1555 the Cortes petitioned the Crown (but vainly) to suppress this literature by a licensing decree. The best minds in Spain deplored the patent degradation of popular taste, but were helpless to stay it. Then it was that Cervantes wrote his immortal satire upon the knight-errant. Like Jonah, the knight de la Mancha is not without elements of greatness. Much of his discourse, when he is free from his obsession, is notable and solid. This, however, only helps to overwhelm with destructive laughter the obsolescent *rôle* he is so anxious to sustain. And in this, the first object of the book, the author is completely successful.

But Cervantes achieved more than an effective criticism of a type of person who, in earlier years, had fulfilled a real function, but whose figure had later become a nuisance and injury to society. What *Don Quixote* did for Spain is put by the late Major Martin Hume thus :

> To other countries that welcomed the marvellous book it appealed by its wit, its satire, and its truth ; and these qualities, together with its pathos, doubtless aided its popularity in Spain also. But to Spaniards

THE BOOK AND THE SIGN 39

it was much more than a witty book; it was the supreme cry, echoing from the inmost heart of the nation, that the old gods were dead, and that Spain's exalted heroics were now but a laughing-stock The nation was indeed decadent · its faith and belief in itself had fled, and presumptuous pretence, personal and national, was but a poor substitute for the spiritual exaltation that had made it great.[1]

Now the *Book of Jonah* does for the professional prophet of the writer's time something like that which *Don Quixote* did for the knight-errant in Spain, only the verdict is not so definitive, even as it is not so stern as the judgement pronounced upon the same lamentable creature in *Zechariah* xiii. The *Book of Jonah* does not banish the prophet either with laughter or with execration, but it makes him a lugubrious renegade, false through cultivated pessimism to the very reason and purpose of his existence. Further, just as *Don Quixote* served also the larger purpose of a judgement upon the Spanish people, so the *Book of Jonah* is more than a criticism of the prophetic order : it condemns the popular mood This will be made more apparent in a later chapter.

We do not know all the causes which led to the presentation of the story of Jonah, as it now stands, but we can see how exceedingly well its parts fit together. In this case a name—the name of the prophet—is certainly more than a mere appellation Israel was often spoken of as a *jonah*, that is, *a dove*[2] The *Son of Amittai* also is a didactic name, suggestively reminding us of Puritan names in Cromwell's day—a period in religious history which resembled the time of our writer in its legalistic conceptions of piety The *Dove* is the *Son of Truth*, the typical guileless and orthodox believer, in the Hebrew community. The actual historic prophet of *II Kings* xiv, 25, who bore this suggestive name, was remembered only as one who had predicted a political expansion of Israel's borders. We may conceive him as concerned more with Israel's

[1] *Cambridge Modern History*, iii, 547.
[2] *Hosea* vii, 11 ; xi, 11.

external greatness than with her spiritual well-being. As such he also contributes to the success of the book that bears his name, for the imperialistic aim in politics, the zeal that seeks an ever-expanding earthly dominion, unhappily is often associated with that dislike of other peoples which is the subject of our writer's censure.

So for those who prided themselves on being strict followers of Moses and Ezra—the Pentateuch was now complete—this allegory of an erring prophet was woven about an old and mostly forgotten man, whose very name seemed framed for the purpose of a deadly satire. In effect the writer said to the prophets of his time and their hearers and associates in the worship of Yahweh . You call yourselves holy. You are harmless as doves, children of impeccable orthodoxy. You believe that God is slow to anger, full of compassion, plenteous in mercy, and that He repents Him of the evil   Yes; you have the whole gamut of the vocabulary of piety. You have had, too, the great lesson of the Exile told you by your fathers   As a nation you have been buried deep in the very belly of Hell. But your temper is unchanged and stiff-necked, and if the word of Yahweh were preached to the Gentiles, and they repented as men never repented before, clothing themselves and even their very sheep and oxen with sackcloth, all mightily, if confusedly, lifting up their crying to Heaven, you would still spurn the Gentiles from fellowship with yourselves, you would refuse to welcome them to share those blessings of which you say so much.

So at least the book could hardly fail to be understood by those to whom especially it was addressed, and who could see its cogency by many a particular or fact of the time which for us is only summarised in the general picture presented by the contemporary literature   Something, perhaps, of the asperity of reproof may have been mitigated by the lambent humour which lights up these few but wonderful pages. This, however, but serves to make its purposive criticism the more unanswerable.

THE BOOK AND THE SIGN 41

And now let us examine yet further this Prophet of the Rueful Countenance, and let the artistic truth of the book establish itself in our minds for noble ends Strange are the contradictions in the thought of the man. *I revere Yahweh*, he says, *the God of Heaven who made both sea and land* Yet rises he up to flee upon the sea *from the Presence of Yahweh*. Indeed three times in the first chapter we are told of Jonah's seeking to flee from the presence of this Universal Creator. Can we disentangle his thoughts, as he hastens down into the ship that is to carry him, he hopes, the whole length of the Mediterranean?

In early times his forefathers in common with other Semites believed animistically. Where we moderns see a reign of universal natural law, they saw things parcelled out and administered by a multitude of spirits In time these supposed beings became a hierarchy under a few chief gods Then every nation possessed its own deity and conversely every deity had its own people and land. Moab belonged to Chemosh, Israel to Yahweh. So when David remonstrated with Saul for hunting him from place to place in the wilderness, he said concerning his enemies, *They have driven me out this day that I should not cleave unto the inheritance of Yahweh, saying, Go, serve other gods. Now therefore let not my blood fall to the earth away from the presence of Yahweh* (*I Samuel* xxvi, 19f.). It would appear from this that across the frontiers of Israel Yahweh's writ did not run. Banishment from the territory of one god meant the transfer of a man's worship to another. So David understood things. It should, perhaps, be added, that here we have the historic David apart from the idealised David, miscredited by tradition with psalms of a far later period. In the same way, the kindred people of Syria once had occasion to say of Israel, *Their god is a god of the hills; therefore they were stronger than we: but let us fight against them in the plain, and surely we shall be stronger than they* (*I Kings* xx, 23). Or again, take this from the story of Naaman the Syrian: convinced of the greatness

D

of Yahweh, Naaman requests of Elisha, *Let there be given to thy servant two mules' burden of earth ; for thy servant will henceforth offer neither burnt-offering nor sacrifice unto other gods, but unto Yahweh* (*II Kings* v, 17). It was just a little bit of Yahweh's land that Naaman needed to take away with him, in order to build an altar to Yahweh in his own country, lying as that did under the rule of a different deity. How otherwise could he worship Yahweh ? But Israel slowly outgrew this common Semitic philosophy of religion, if we may call it such. The splendid faith of the eighth century prophets claimed a wider jurisdiction for Yahweh. Amos demands for Him, *Are ye not as the children of the Ethiopians unto me, O children of Israel ? saith the Lord. Have not I brought up Israel out of the land of Egypt, and the Philistines from Caphtor, and the Syrians from Kir ?* (*Amos* ix, 7). The circumstances of the time, however, compelled Isaiah to emphasise the presence of Yahweh in His temple at Jerusalem, and from that emphasis sprang a great evil. A ritual-and-magic-loving generation shut up its faith within those temple walls. All the tragedy of the Exile had its source in the demoralising of religion which then followed. But once again, as so often in the systolic and diastolic movements of Revelation came a new breath into Israel's soul. As out of the broken chrysalis there rises a higher-ranked creature than the caterpillar that had slumbered there, so out of the broken walls of Jerusalem's temple arose a fairer and more spiritual religion than any previous generation had known. The faith of Israel was emancipated from territorialism. In the Babylonian captivity the Hebrew was driven to seek God without even the help of Naaman's two mules' burden of sacred earth, without holy buildings, altars, or sacrifices. Three happily consecutive psalms of the Exile period, or a little later, the 137th, 138th and 139th[1] record the result. At first all was mournful perplexity:

[1] The titles of the 138th and 139th are, as so often in the Psalter, misleading and should be ignored.

THE BOOK AND THE SIGN

By the rivers of Babylon,
There we sat down, yea, we wept
When we remembered Zion.
Upon the willows in the midst thereof
We hanged up our harps.
For there they that led us captive required of us songs,
And they that wasted us required of us mirth, saying,
Sing us one of the songs of Zion.
How shall we sing Yahweh's Song
In a strange land? (cxxxvii, 1-4).

Aye, that was the problem, man's perpetually recurring problem, the problem of the transplanting of worship from the dear, familiar, sacred haunts of the Past into some forbidding territory of the unknown and the unexplored. But man's very need as he sits among his broken theologies compels a rebirth of trust in a mightier God. The 138th Psalm answers the 137th:

I will give thee thanks with my whole heart:
Before the gods will I sing praises unto thee.

Before the Gods. Conspicuously before the Gods, runs the Hebrew verse (נֶגֶד אֱלֹהִים), *will I sing praises unto thee. All the kings of the earth shall give thee thanks, O Yahweh.*

Surely that was a splendid defiance of deities, the singing of Yahweh's praises right in their very faces! It meant that for the worshipper these traditional gods, the supposed guardians of foreign lands, were fading into powerless ghosts, like shreds of the night mists a summer dawn disperses, and that with their evanescence the whole wide world was Yahweh's land.

Finally, the writer of the 139th Psalm registers as with a gasp of wonder the advance thus made in Hebrew thinking:

O Yahweh, thou hast searched me and known me.
Thou knowest my downsitting and mine uprising,
Thou understandest my thought afar off.

* * * * *

> *Thou hast beset me behind and before,*
> *And laid thine hand upon me.*
> *Such knowledge is too wonderful for me;*
> *It is high, I cannot attain unto it.*
> *Whither shall I go from thy spirit?*
> *Or whither shall I flee from thy presence?*
> *If I ascend up into heaven, thou art there.*
> *If I take the wings of the morning,*
> *And dwell in the uttermost parts of the sea;*
> *Even there shall thy hand lead me,*
> *And thy right hand shall hold me.*

Such was the faith reached by Israel in Babylon. With that revelation the Exiles returned. The men and women around the author of the *Book of Jonah* were supposed to hold this larger creed. Indeed, as we have seen Jonah himself testifies to it in his confession to the sailors on board the ship. Jonah knows it all and prays to his God from the very belly of the fish, deep down at the bottom of the sea, knowing that even there Yahweh's right hand can hold him and lift him out. Is it not strange that sharing the splendour of Israel's enlarged faith, this man, because of rooted aversion to the task imposed upon him, should have turned back to the older, narrower faith of Yahweh and His land, and have seriously thought that he could escape the God who had been so vastly revealed? It is an illustration of lines in Francis Thompson's *The Hound of Heaven:*

> I fled Him down the arches of the years;
> I fled Him down the labyrinthine ways
> Of my own mind.

The secret of this lapse into an earlier theology is just Jonah's very refusal to express the larger faith of his people in missionary service. For if Yahweh be the World-God, He claims sovereignty and dispenses grace in Nineveh as well as in Jerusalem. But it is always true that he who disobeys the practical implications of a great creed loses the glory he has seen therein, and is drawn back through

THE BOOK AND THE SIGN

the arches of the years and the labyrinthine ways of his own mind into the old discredited limitations he had outgrown! The half-truths and the half-gods set up their thrones in our own hearts with incredible swiftness and insolent familiarity, when we are false to the larger religion of the universal God. That is a great saying of the Frenchman, Turgot, in the eighteenth century: " It is not error which opposes the progress of Truth "—or we might add, the retention of truth—" it is indolence, obstinacy, the spirit of routine, everything that favours inaction."

VI

THE BOOK AS PROPAGANDA

VI

THE BOOK AS PROPAGANDA

THE common mind of the Church, which has collected for us and sent forth as authoritative Scripture the sixty-six books of the Old and the New Testament, is so manifestly of God, that Christian people ought never to despair of a superintending Providence working through all the changes of their opinions. The catholicity of the collection is extraordinary. Here, side by side, lie books and pamphlets which, at least on their surface, plainly disagree. The disagreements are all the more impressive in that there is nothing bitter about them The sacred writers were content merely to state opposite aspects of Truth. They shewed respect to the prerogatives of our individual minds by leaving to us the task of reconciliation. Indeed nothing in the Bible is more suggestive of the potential oneness of God and Man than this Divine employment of writers antipodean to each other. For to each of us, on whose behalf this high employ is devised, God clearly calls saying, as to His servant Ezekiel, *Son of man, stand upon thy feet, and I will speak with thee*[1] This erect attitude, with *loins girt like a man*, is the condition in which His truth is best apprehended, whether offered us in the Old Testament[2] or in the New.[3]

In our present study, concerned only with Hebrew Scriptures, what antithetical positions are disclosed! The broad oppositions of Law and Prophecy are familiar to

[1] *Ezekiel* ii, 1.
[2] *Job* xxxviii, 3; xl, 7.
[3] *I Peter* i, 13.

every student. How far apart, again, is the prudential righteousness of *Proverbs* from the superb self-integrity of the patriarch Job! Or again, to turn from the *Song of Songs* to *Ecclesiastes*, its immediate predecessor in the order of the books, is like making a magic transposition from some tropical island of luxuriant beauty to the austere loveliness of an antarctic summer; yet both Scriptures are of God. And, amongst the prophets, *Nahum* and the *Book of Jonah* deal with the same guilty people of Nineveh, but in manners how different! Two brief booklets, one numbering forty-seven verses, the other forty-eight, they might suitably be printed in parallel columns, in illustration of that diversity of operation which is wrought by the one Spirit.

The wickedness from which the *Book of Jonah* represents the Ninevites repenting is rhetorically described in *Nahum* thus: *Where is the den of the lions, and the feeding place of the young lions, where the lion and the lioness walked, the lion's whelp, and none made them afraid? The lion did tear in pieces enough for his whelps, and strangled for his lionesses, and filled his caves with prey, and his dens with ravin* (ii, 11, 12). *Woe to the bloody city! it is all full of lies and rapine; the prey departeth not* (iii, 1). . . . *There is no assuaging of thy hurt; thy wound is grievous: all that hear the bruit of thee clap the hands over thee; for upon whom hath not thy wickedness passed continually?* (iii, 19) If we need any confirmation of Nahum's accusations against Nineveh we have only to read the books of the Assyrian kings themselves in their clay tablet libraries and monuments. Summing up these Prof. Sayce declares that on the capture of a town

> Pyramids of human heads marked the path of the conqueror; boys and girls were burned alive or reserved for a worse fate; men were impaled, flayed alive, blinded, or deprived of their hands and feet, of their ears and noses, while the women and children were carried into slavery, the captured city plundered

THE BOOK AND THE SIGN 51

and reduced to ashes, and the trees in its neighbourhood cut down.[1]

Such was the wickedness of which Yahweh's word to Jonah said—*it has affronted me*. We can understand Nahum's exaltation when Nineveh itself was trampled down by the enemy. We are tempted to say with *Rabbi Ben Ezra*,

This rage was right i' the main.

Was it not a right desire to see the vindication of justice upon the earth? Even enlightened Christian teachers, like Richard Baxter in *The Saints' Everlasting Rest*,[2] remembering the wantonness and cruelties of their times, have fiercely craved a sight of Hell for the enhancement of the joys of Heaven.

Now the author of the *Book of Jonah* doubtless chose Nineveh as his theme just because its reputation had been so vile All that Nahum felt he also may have felt. In any case Nahum wrote some centuries before him. Was he a reader of Nahum's scroll? Did this pæan of rejoicing over Nineveh's fate, however righteously motived, seem to him too perilous an emotion for the men of his day, restless already under a similar heathen yoke? Did he see how those sins are commonly accounted the worst which happen to hurt their judges the most? Certainly righteous indignation is always a most unmanageable virtue. While without it we may readily draw upon ourselves the rebuke of a wise writer,

*As a troubled fountain, and a corrupted spring,
So is a righteous man that giveth way before the wicked*,[3]

yet the dangers of resentment are grave. Shakespeare has shewn us the progress of anger in *Timon of Athens*. Here is one who by loss of fortune learns too late the unworthiness of friendships based upon mere cupidity. Turning

[1] *Assyria: its Princes, Priests and People*, p 127.
[2] Cf chap. V, 111. Cf also Augustine's *City of God*, Bk XX, chap 22, etc, etc.
[3] *Proverbs* xxv, 26.

with legitimate wrath from his ungrateful associates, Timon falls a prey to that egotistic spirit ever lurking in human nature, which is apt haughtily to demand for us the unique deference of our fellows. It is not long before this disillusioned man is heaping curses upon the whole population of Athens. Like Jonah sitting outside Nineveh watching and still hoping for its overthrow, Timon haunts the woods beyond the city's wall desiring nothing but evil to befall it. From such a mood it is only a step to this—

> And grant as Timon grows, his hate may grow
> To the whole race of mankind, high and low!
> Amen.

Difficult is it for men to obey the apostolic admonition, *Be ye angry and sin not*.

The attitude of Nahum and of Nehemiah, and then later again that of the Maccabees, towards the Gentile world hardened yet further as the hope of political freedom died away. While, in the time of Christ, Judaism outside Palestine, was not without, to use Professor Harnack's phrase, 'the feeling that self-diffusion was a duty,'[1] the opposite tendency characterised more especially the Judaism of Jerusalem. We see an illustration of this when S. Paul, defending himself before the people was led to narrate his vision of the risen Jesus and to affirm, *He said unto me, Depart: for I will send thee forth far hence unto the Gentiles.* Then we read, *And they gave him audience unto this word*—Gentiles—*and they lifted up their voice, and said, Away with such a fellow from the earth: for it is not fit that he should live.*[2] We recall the verdict of Tacitus upon them, 'Connected amongst themselves by the most obstinate and inflexible faith, the Jews extend their charity to all of their own persuasion, while towards the rest of mankind they nourish a sullen and inveterate hatred.'[3]

---

[1] See *The Mission and Expansion of Christianity*, i, 15ff.
[2] *The Acts* xxii, 21f.
[3] *History*, V, 5.

THE BOOK AND THE SIGN 53

That may be a judgement more of scorn than of truth, but it accords only too well with other testimonies.

Indignation at sin easily passes into dislike of sinners, and dislike of sinners into that enmity which at last merits Shelley's incisive phrase, " eyeless with hate." Professor Dowden has commented upon the beauty and worthiness of the character of Timon's steward in the play, and he adds, " this his Master, blinded by his fierce misanthropy, has no eyes to see."[1] So Jonah, corroded in spirit by hatred of his country's oppressors, has no eyes for the simple humanity of the sailors, whose lives he knows he has imperilled, and who yet seek so earnestly to save him from the threatening doom of his God. Nor does the spectacle of a nation upon its knees quicken his pity. He fails to see how God has been moving in their hearts. He has forgotten Yahweh's word through Amos, *Have not I brought up the Philistines from Caphtor, and the Syrians from Kir ?* He has lost that clue to national suffering, which the great prophet of the Exile had set forth in the Song of the Suffering Servant of Yahweh (*Isaiah* lii, 13—liii), who puts away the guilt of the heathen races by the offering of himself. " He is eyeless with hate." But also he is ridiculous and this is the point of the propaganda.

[1] *Shakspere Primer*, p 144.

VII

THE ANATOMY OF BIGOTRY

VII

THE ANATOMY OF BIGOTRY

IF the *Book of Jonah* was written and sent upon its way in ancient Israel, both by oral circulation and by the fast multiplying copies of scribes, not only to beget amongst the common people a kindlier attitude to the nations without the law—the " lesser breeds," as our own Imperialist poet calls them—but especially to rebuke the deadening bigotry of the professional exponents of Hebrew religion, it will be worth our while in the present chapter to examine the kind of bigotry which the writer had in view and to search out, if we can, its causes.

Bigotry is a disease which takes many forms. It has been described by Prof J Clark Murray as " the moral characteristic which combines strong will with narrow intelligence in its direction "[1] That is a description which may be correctly applied to Jonah He is certainly possessed of strength of will. He argues in the face of his God, adhering to his own gloomy mood despite all the Divine correction. He says, as men of his type always do say, sourly enough, " I told you so Was not this my saying ? I have not altered my mind " He forgets nothing and apparently learns nothing Hence his intelligence remains closely restricted in outlook.

Now such would seem to have been the character of that generation of Jewish people who with indomitable pluck set their hands to the rebuilding of Jerusalem and

[1] Article in *The Encyclopædia of Religion and Ethics*, ii, 618.

the surrounding country   No one can withhold admiration from Nehemiah and the men he led, as, notwithstanding persistent opposition, and amid all the discouragements of poverty, they set themselves to restore the land of their fathers. Yet it remains true that they turned the drift of Israel's religious life into a channel that narrowed more and more   The influence of Ezra and his companions led to the exaltation of the Law and to a consequent glorifying of the priest and the scribe   During the Persian period came the establishment of synagogues throughout the country. This offered the opportunity of spiritualising religion by the introduction of regular spoken addresses. But the opportunity was largely lost   The Law was made the one supreme object of exposition and this so effectually that its supremacy remains to the present day   Maimonides, the most famous of Jewish philosophers—he died in A.D. 1204—is quoted approvingly by M. Friedlander in these terms · " It has been distinctly stated in the Torah that its precepts remain in force for ever without change, diminution, or addition.   . Hence we see that a prophet cannot reveal any new law "[1]   Modern Liberal Judaism may, indeed, take a broader outlook than this, but Liberal Judaism has yet to vindicate itself before the great majority of religious Jews

Now the Torah (i e , the Pentateuch) certainly embraces many valuable elements besides its laws and rules, but it has too little poetry to be an adequate instrument of a full religious training ; moreover it has been the legal element in the Torah which more than anything else has attracted the study of orthodox Judaism. Herein lay the chief defect of synagogue piety. Its emphasis was wrong. It lacked Idealism. Poetry humanises   Music and Imagination are the wings of Faith, and Faith takes the soul as with a plunge into the Immensities that redeem us   Any religious judgement, therefore, which assigns to Prophecy and Poetry a lower degree of inspiration than that claimed

[1] *The Jewish Religion* (published 1891) p 217

THE BOOK AND THE SIGN 59

for Law is bound to develop an unlovely spirit Sympathy, so vital to comprehensive views of human nature, finds little quickening in legalism. Insight and hope alike decay, while the more sternly a man seeks to walk by rule, the less charitable he generally becomes So it was that the neo-Ezraism of the fifth century B C grew ever harder. It was not merely, as our last chapter may have suggested, that Israel's sufferings at the hands of heathen powers embittered her. The Law became an instrument of alienation from humanity The outside world not allowed to share Hebrew altars was spurned also as a world of enemies and fools *Remember this*, cries a Psalmist, *the enemy doth reproach An impudent people do contemn Thy name*.[1] Gradually bigotry reached its full height.

But when we attempt the Anatomy of Bigotry it is not enough to lay bare the conditions under which it has reared its rank shape. We must dig deeper and discover its ultimate root.

Lovers of English literature will recognise the origin of the title of this chapter in a famous work greatly beloved by Samuel Johnson. *The Anatomy of Melancholy*, by Robert Burton, a seventeenth century Anglican clergyman of immense learning, has a section upon Bigotry, its character and cure The writer finds no bigotry in the Church to which he belongs but plenty of it in the Romanists and Separatists of his time " What," he exclaims, " are all our Anabaptists, Brownists, Barrowists, Familists, but a company of rude, illiterate, capricious, base fellows ? What are most of our Papists but stupid, ignorant and blind bayards ? how should they otherwise be, when they are brought up and kept still in darkness ? . . . Being so misled all their lives in superstition, and carried hoodwinked like hawks how can they prove otherwise than blind idiots and superstitious asses ? " (part iii, sec. 4) This is written by way of reproving Bigotry The cure of

[1] *Psalm* lxxiv, 18. *International Critical Commentary* translation

Bigotry is then set down with equal vigour and clearness, " For the vulgar, restrain them by laws, mulcts, burn their books, forbid their conventicles , for when the cause is taken away, the effect will soon cease. Now for prophets, dreamers, and for such rude, silly fellows, that through fasting, too much meditation, preciseness, or by melancholy are distempered ; the best means to reduce them *ad sanam mentem*, is to alter their course of life, and with conference, threats, promises, persuasions, to intermix physic . . I think the compendious cure, for some of them at least, had been in Bedlam "

Now if some suggestions in the Anatomy and for the cure of Bigotry may be attempted in this chapter, they must not be exactly on Burton's lines. Yet, if we may ignore his glaring *petitio principii* throughout his polemic against Rome and the Protestant denominations, there is truth in his criticism Bigotry, he seems to say, arises from poverty of life. Neo-Ezraism illustrates that contention

The root-cause of the great failure of post-exilic Israel to attain any noble religious outlook was deeper than legalism and scribalism. The entire life of the period was thin and poor. Herein it would appear to be with the community as it is with the individual. Adolescence, when life, physical and intellectual, is surging up in the person, is generally the time of religious enthusiasm. And history shows us that great moments of national revival in piety are generally moments when the common life of the time is full The late Dr McEwen in his *History of the Church in Scotland* (Vol II) has a striking chapter entitled " Scotland in Renaissance," which bears upon this matter. He exhibits the epoch of the Reformation in Scotland as a time when in politics, municipal affairs and social life there was a great ferment working The lower orders of the nobility and the gentry were claiming a larger place in politics. The burgh was developing both in vitality and in organisation, and the artisans were seeking a share in its concerns. Foreign trade was bringing into the country

THE BOOK AND THE SIGN 61

wealth of ideas as well as wealth of goods Finally the peasantry were awakening to their rights and opportunities. There was, in short, a renaissance of the nation as a whole, and the reform of the church was part of a great uprush of life in the national consciousness We may add, what was true of Scotland was true of the reforming peoples generally.

Now at such a time Bigotry is not a characteristic vice. It may be a transmitted discoloration from less spacious days, but each new wave of life tends to widen the outlook by strengthening the optic nerve of the mind, so bringing into view all the hinterlands that adjoin our creeds. In a season like this Nehemiahs do not go about cursing and plucking off the hair of those who have connexions with foreigners, nor do Jonahs watch hungrily for the destruction of hereditary foes.

Conversely, Bigotry is always the brazen front of misgiving it is the bluff of weakness, the blotch in the flesh which reveals anæmia in the blood Sophocles in the *Antigone* puts the matter thus, " Wear not, then, one mood only in thyself , think not that thy word and thine alone must be right For if any man thinks that he alone is wise,—that in speech, or in mind, he hath no peer, such a soul, when laid open, is ever found empty "[1] And this is specially true of that particular type of Bigotry which the *Book of Jonah* exhibits—the refusal to admit the pariah peoples to our fellowship in Divine things. It is more than dislike of the foreigner which animates us It is the self-deceiving misgiving heart within us, whose supreme ailment is vacuity. We refuse to speak of God to those who need Him only when we have really nothing to tell. We shut our souls against the mute appeal of a seeking world only when there is nothing within them to guard. We have only words of judgement for the outsider because we ourselves are strangers to grace We brandish conventional phrases of theology to hide a bankrupt religion.

If we consider the poor, straitened character of that

[1] Lines 707-9 Sir Richard Jebb's translation.

little highland subject-state which Ezra, Nehemiah, Haggai and Zechariah built, we must admit that the *tout-ensemble* was not impressive. Even in the case of the leaders themselves the Spirit of God had, relatively, poor stuff to work upon. Not for one moment can you put them alongside the great prophets and kings of the eighth century. Theirs was a day of small things ; they were small people ; and some of them knew it.

Where then does the cure of Bigotry lie ? One seems to descry a helpless conclusion. Is it that we must wait until the hidden cisterns mysteriously fill up again, and life comes flooding in once more with its surge of adventure and expansion and hope ? If so, character is determined for us and no place is left for praise or blame. Is there no way but this ?

We shall find our answer as we study life more closely and watch its laws of gift and renewal. Let us hear what a modern thinker has to say upon biological phenomena. In his *Creative Evolution* M. Henri Bergson declares :—

> Life in general is mobility itself ; particular manifestations of life accept this mobility reluctantly, and constantly lag behind. It is always going ahead; they want to mark time. Evolution in general would fain go on in a straight line ; each special evolution is a kind of circle. Like eddies of dust raised by the wind as it passes, the living turn upon themselves, borne up by the great blast of life. They are therefore relatively stable, and counterfeit immobility so well that we treat each of them as a *thing* rather than as a *progress*, forgetting that the very permanence of their form is only the outline of a movement. At times, however, in a fleeting vision, the invisible breath that bears them is materialised before our eyes. We have this sudden illumination before certain forms of maternal love, so striking and in most animals so touching, observable even in the solicitude of the plant for its seed. This love, in which some have seen the great mystery of life, may possibly deliver us

THE BOOK AND THE SIGN

life's secret. It shows us each generation leaning over the generation that shall follow It allows us a glimpse of the fact that *the living being is above all a thoroughfare, and that the essence of life is in the movement by which life is transmitted* [1]

More recently in an essay upon the "Psychology of Power" a medical specialist has said ·

> Nature is economic in her gifts: she will not give strength to those who will not expend it. These remain uninspiring and uninspired She is lavish in her gifts to those who will use them, and especially to those who devote them to nature's altruistic ends, for such ends harmonise the soul Life demands expression. If the life-stream that flows through us finds the channel blocked by a life of inactivity, we inevitably suffer from staleness and boredom, or a sense of physical debility. . . . We are not merely receptacles but *channels* of energy. Life and power is not so much contained in us, it *courses through* us [2]

If these teachings are true—and does not something of the very genius of Christian experience attest them?—the remedy for low vitality with all its attendant evils must lie in our beginning to give, even though what we have to give is but the widow's handful of meal and drop of oil in the cruse. Does not that touch the root of the matter? Turn back from Jonah's booth outside Nineveh and scrutinize the Church in the homeland he had left Somewhere in Jerusalem itself did there not lie unconsecrated possessions? Did not "the particular manifestations" of life "lag behind" Life itself? It is good sometimes to employ the great phrases of inherited creeds, but in Religion quotation is always a suspect process For, as Henry Suso wrote, "There was never a string so dulcet-toned but ceased to sound if stretched to a withered frame; a heart poor in love can no more understand speech rich in love than a

---
[1] pp 134-5. italics in the last sentence are mine
[2] Dr J. A. Hadfield, in *The Spirit* (pp. 104 and 111).

German can an Italian"[1] *A gracious God, full of compassion, slow to anger, plenteous in mercy, repenting of the evil*—how far did these historic watchwords awaken responsive devotion not to Nineveh's need, but even to that of Jerusalem ? how far were they even understood ? *Malachi*, a work certainly earlier than *Jonah*, but belonging to the same religious epoch, tells a story of worship which had become an acknowledged weariness, a slovenly routine,

> Still pumping phrases for the Ineffable,
> Though all the valves of memory gasp and wheeze,

—a story of lame and sick animals given to Yahweh, as to-day the well-to-do send their cast clothes to the jumble-sales of the poor,—a polluted table and tithes of the storehouse withheld (*Malachi* 1, 7 , iii, 8) Was it wonderful there was no grace for Nineveh when Jerusalem fared so ill ? Yet the power to give was there

It is within our own reach to rise into newness of life. However weak and low we may be, however impoverished all the other spheres of our time—industry, merchandise, literature, art—the way to renewal is by gift of what we have, and it is the failure to give which hands us over to all manner of pettinesses, squabbles and misanthropies. And while religious quickening may often arise, as we have seen it has arisen, through the increase of the whole life of the time, it is too Divine a thing to be wholly determined by external conditions The soul is constructed for autonomy and for immediate access to God. Man is child of the Infinite and Eternal

Further, it does not so much matter where contact may function, whether in Nineveh or Jerusalem, in foreign mission or home ministry , essential religion means our sublimation into God Where that happens universal love is born in the soul As Thomas Traherne teaches us, communion with God means a real union of the human with the Divine in all the largeness of the Divine activity

---

[1] Cf Dr Otto's *The Idea of the Holy*, English Edition, p. 48.

THE BOOK AND THE SIGN

" God willed," he says, " the redemption of mankind and therefore is His Son Jesus Christ an infinite treasure to you. Verily you ought to will these things so ardently that God Himself should be therefore your joy because He willed them *Your will ought to be united to His in all places of His dominion . . . Woulds't thou love God alone ? God alone cannot be beloved.* . He must be loved in all with an unlimited love, even in all His doings, in all His friends, in all His creatures Everywhere in all things thou must meet His love "[1] What Traherne means by our being united to God in all places of His dominion may be illustrated by the exquisite thought (not necessarily pantheistic) of Shelley in his lament over the death of John Keats ·

> He is made one with Nature . there is heard
> His voice in all her music, from the moan
> Of thunder to the song of night's sweet bird ;
> He is a presence to be felt and known
> In darkness and in light, from herb and stone,
> Spreading itself where'er that Power may move
> Which has withdrawn his being to its own ;
> Which wields the world with never wearied love,
> Sustains it from beneath, and kindles it above.

Yes · but even before " Death with the might of his sunbeam " liberates us into this ampler life, the soul that knows communion with God blends itself into all His vast compassions, and realises that it can never know His love towards itself, apart from His redeeming grace to others. The Universal's love breathes universality into the one beloved

And no man knows God thus who withholds aught from Him. The altar fires of Jerusalem must burn luminously with Israel's choicest offerings, or there will be no abiding vision of world-salvation, no message for Nineveh but pitiless doom

---
[1] *Centuries of Meditations*, 1, 53 and 72 Italics mine

VIII

THE SIGN OF JONAH

VIII

THE SIGN OF JONAH

ACCORDING to *S. Matthew* our Lord twice spoke of Jonah as a sign For the first reference we have a parallel in *S. Luke*, and the second belongs to a passage also found in *S. Mark* We may dismiss this second reference (*S Matthew* xvi, 1-4 *S. Mark* viii, 11-13) from our present consideration, since it tells us nothing beyond what is indicated in the earlier one.

In seeking an explanation of the Sign of Jonah we must first of all compare the two narratives, which run as follows ·

S Matthew xii, 38-42	*S Luke* xi, 29-32
Then certain of the scribes and Pharisees answered him, saying, Master, we would see a sign from thee But he answered and said unto them, An evil and adulterous generation seeketh after a sign, and there shall no sign be given to it but the sign of Jonah the prophet for as Jonah was three days and three nights in the belly of the whale, so shall the Son of man be three days and three nights in the heart of the earth. The men of Nineveh shall stand up in the judgement with this generation, and shall condemn it, for they repented at the preaching of Jonah, and behold, a greater than Jonah is here The queen of the south shall rise up in the judgement with this generation, and shall condemn it for she came from the ends of the earth to hear the wisdom of Solomon, and behold, a greater than Solomon is here	And when the multitudes were gathering together unto him, he began to say, This generation is an evil generation it seeketh after a sign, and there shall no sign be given to it but the sign of Jonah For even as Jonah became a sign unto the Ninevites, so shall also the Son of man be to this generation The queen of the south shall rise up in the judgement with the men of this generation, and shall condemn them for she came from the ends of the earth to hear the wisdom of Solomon, and behold, a greater than Solomon is here The men of Nineveh shall stand up in the judgement with this generation, and shall condemn it for they repented at the preaching of Jonah, and behold, a greater than Jonah is here

It will be observed that whereas both Gospels speak of Jonah as a sign, in *S Matthew* Jonah is a sign to our Lord's own generation, in *S. Luke* he was a sign to the Ninevites first, and it is as such he suggests a parallel to the significance of Jesus. Then there emerges a further notable difference. *S. Luke* is content merely to speak of Jonah as a sign without telling us what he signified. *S Matthew* expounds the sign as a foreshadowing of the Burial and, by implication, the Resurrection of Jesus *For as Jonah was three days and three nights in the belly of the whale, so shall the Son of man be three days and three nights in the heart of the earth* The question arises, Did our Lord actually say this or did He leave the sign comparatively unexplained as in *S Luke*? If He expounded the sign in the way *S. Matthew* describes, how comes it that *S Luke* omits this exposition? The suggestion of certain writers that *S. Luke's* version of the words is a summary report of that in *S. Matthew* is open to two objections. In the first place *S. Luke* does not follow *S. Matthew's* order of the verses respecting the men of Nineveh and the Queen of Sheba, although here *S Matthew* clearly has the more likely sequence of thought, so that the writer can hardly have had *S. Matthew's* narrative, or *S. Matthew's* source before him. In the second place, the author of the third Gospel had no motive for ruling out of the discourse anything which emphasised a miracle. No anti-miraculous feeling is discernible in his work elsewhere, and if, as is probable, he was none other than S. Paul's *beloved physician*, he belonged to a profession which in those days was rather too much disposed to accept stories of the supernatural than otherwise. Had *S Matthew's* form of the saying been before him when he wrote, it is highly improbable that he would have rejected it in favour of a more general version of his own. I conclude, therefore, that the two versions are mutually independent, and it remains for us to choose which of the two we should accept as a report of what our Lord actually said.

THE BOOK AND THE SIGN

In estimating the value of S. *Matthew's* version one has to remember a special influence to which the writer of this Gospel was exposed, perhaps more fully than was the case with S. *Luke*. In early Christian circles, as Dr Rendel Harris has lately shewn us, there was circulated a *Testimony Book*, used more especially for the confutation of Jewish unbelievers This work embodied certain Old Testament passages that were supposed to prefigure Christ, and applied them to various incidents in the Evangelic tradition. It is quite likely that the *Book of Jonah* would be drawn upon in this way In any case the influence of the *Testimony Book* would point the direction of the evangelist's thinking. Puzzled, perhaps, as to the meaning of our Saviour's words and so turning back to the *Book of Jonah* to see in what respects a parallel to Jesus was to be found therein, it would flash upon him that the reference may have been to the prophet's incarceration in the great fish for three days and three nights. He would have no scruple in amplifying our Lord's words so as to include his own edifying interpretation of them, for in such a free manner of composition contemporary canons of literary workmanship found no matter for offence. Nor would it appear a difficulty to him that apparently, according to the later development of his own story, Jesus was not in the heart of the earth for three days and three nights, but for about half that time. Jewish methods of reckoning days and hours may have permitted Matthew to make his statement without obvious inaccuracy In any case a broad comparison between the lot of Jonah in the belly of the whale and the lot of Jesus in the heart of the earth was near enough to enable the evangelist to conclude that the *Sign of Jonah* here found its interpretation.

The great difficulty, however, in the way of our acceptance of S. *Matthew's* Version is that in the first place it is self-contradictory, and, in the second place, is alien to the general method of our Lord's teaching Does not Jesus expressly declare that no sign should be given to that evil

and adulterous generation but the sign of Jonah ? Why
should He make this exception whilst refusing every other
sign ? Is it not just because of its enigmatic quality?
He would be stultifying Himself surely if after giving it
to His heckling questioners He proceeded to particularise
it as a marvel. Again, throughout His ministry He re-
pudiated the carnal appetite for wonders Yet in the class
of popular marvels anything more truly sensational than a
man's three days' burial and subsequent resurrection could
hardly be conceived And it is wholly in keeping with this
that, in the Providence of God, all the actual manifestations
of the risen Saviour were withheld from those who in His
mortal life had so often clamoured for signs, and were
granted only to *witnesses that were chosen before of God*,[1] in
other words, to those only who, as trained spiritually by
Jesus, were fitted to behold Him This, as I have already
suggested, was not the only occasion upon which our Lord
deprecated the appeal to the Supernatural [2] It was not,
of course, that He doubted the existence of a world beyond
what we call Nature, or had any merely faint conception of
its powers. That world was never far away from His
thoughts But He knew that man's loyalty to Truth ever
requires an economy in the use of the appeal to the supernatural He never attempted the impossible method of
bludgeoning the soul with the dead weight of the inexpli-
cable into an acceptance of spiritual realities And His
attitude in these grave concerns has always approved itself
to the best minds amongst us M Maeterlinck strikes the
same note in his *Mary Magdalene* when, referring to the
report of the raising of Lazarus, one of the characters in
the play says of Jesus :

> If he can convince me that I have acted wrong until
> to-day, I will amend, for I seek only the truth. But,
> if all the dead who people these valleys were to rise
> from their graves to bear witness, in his name, to a

[1] *The Acts* x, 41
[2] See, e g , *S Luke* xvi, 31

THE BOOK AND THE SIGN

truth less high than that which I know, I would not believe them. Whether the dead sleep or wake, I will not give them a thought unless they teach me to make a better use of my life.

If we needed any further evidence for the rejection of S. Matthew's explanation we should surely find it in the fact that Jesus commonly refused to explain to *them that are without* (the kingdom) the meaning of the symbols and parables He employed.[1] Such refusal was based upon His governing conception of the method of human salvation. Men must themselves seek, think, pray, and this with the striving of the athlete. Jesus was no party to such a simplification of the Gospel as, in the supposed interests of human weakness, would encourage any abdication of the individual mind. He would flash upon his hearers the light of a magic phrase such as the *Sign of Jonah* and leave to their hearts and consciences the doing of that spectrum-analysis work, whereby its various lessons might be discerned.[2]

We are free therefore to turn our attention to the saying in its original greatness unrestricted by the apologetic particularism of the first Gospel. In what sense then, was Jonah, as S. Luke puts it, *a sign to the Ninevites?* How did Jesus conceive this significance?

Now, our Lord had a way of reading the Old Testament which was distinctly His own. This was apparent to the earliest disciples *He taught them as one having authority* —the authority of spiritual insight—*and not as their scribes.* In His use of any Scripture He does not appear to have considered, as we are wont to do, the exact purpose of its author. The Old Testament Scriptures for Him were the

---

[1] S. Matthew xiii, 10ff. S. Mark iv, 11.
[2] As we thus feel compelled to reject S. Matthew's version of our Lord's words, so also in a somewhat similar case—the passage *Destroy this temple*, in S. John ii, 18ff —we must discriminate between the words there attributed to Jesus and the Evangelist's comment upon them. His words are capable of an interpretation different both from that of the Jews and that of the Evangelist.

oracles of God, and the Spirit of God in Himself could be trusted to reveal God's meanings to Him. To us that Spirit in Jesus seems to follow a path differing widely from some forms of undoubted inspiration in the West. Jesus had the poetic temperament which sees ideas in concrete things, symbols in history, parables everywhere. It is an imaginative mind which can exclaim, *I beheld Satan fallen as lightning from Heaven*, or again, summing up in three words a story of terrific moral import, *Remember Lot's wife*.

When, therefore, Jesus thought of the story of Jonah, other considerations than those we are wont to entertain would be likely to present themselves. Questions as to the place of the book in literature certainly did not trouble Him. Nor did He concern Himself with the purpose of the author [1]. But He followed with eagerness the adventures of Jonah—would it not be one of His boyhood's favourite stories? He saw the man in the midst of the godless city, saw him with all that wonderful thought-vividness which enabled Jesus so often to speak unforgettable words. It should be noted that although the allusion He makes to Jonah is followed by a reference to the prophet's preaching and to the consequent repentance of the Ninevites, more was evidently in our Lord's mind than Jonah's preaching. And for the moment He saw him not in his misanthropy, as the author intended him to be seen, but as a great man. For when Jesus declared, *A greater than Jonah is here* He certainly affirmed of the prophet a commanding personal value. The man was great enough to be a sign to thousands. What, then, was the kind of greatness Jesus discerned in him? We may be sure He did not lose sight of the underlying patriotism and feeling for justice, which motived so often Hebrew antagonism to the nations that oppressed, not Israel alone, but all the lesser peoples. Such affections not only accord with personal greatness but are essential to the noblest character. Jonah had these. When he spoke of *my own*

[1] See, further, Note C on p. 100.

THE BOOK AND THE SIGN

land (iv, 2) he revealed the drift of a deep devotion, however previously submerged by indolence, if such had been his fault. When he ran the risk of a violent death in the streets of Nineveh, by denouncing God's doom upon its citizens, he shewed a physical courage which is one of the elementary virtues of manhood. This also Jesus, who Himself led a menaced life, would not be likely to overlook. But in our Lord's view of him such qualities as these would, I think, be subsumed beneath a more distinctly religious aspect. For the purpose of describing this let us look once more at the story of the book and make an instructive comparison with another great work of literature

The *Book of Jonah* might almost be called a sailor's book The salt of the sea is in its pages   The picture of the storm reminds us of the opening scene in *The Tempest* where, as on the Tartessus ship, the sailors' cry goes up,

All lost, to prayers, to prayers, all lost.

In true nautical manner is the saying about the straining vessel, she *reckoned herself doomed* (1, 5)   The great sea-monster that swallows the prophet belongs to that strange sailors' world, in which to this very day common sights and sounds sometimes give place to the supernatural and the weird

Now we have in English literature another great sea-story, the plot of which revolves upon the sinful deed of one man, just as the storm in the *Book of Jonah* follows upon one man's dereliction of duty   I mean, of course, Coleridge's *Ancient Mariner*

> It is an ancient Mariner,
> And he stoppeth one of three.
> " By thy long grey beard and glittering eye,
> Now wherefore stopp'st thou me ? "
>   * * * * *
> He holds him with his glittering eye—
> The wedding-guest stood still,
> And listens like a three years' child :
> The Mariner hath his will,

Coleridge makes his man of the sea *a sign* to the wedding-guest. The awful scenes the mariner had been through, the mystery of the sea, its rotting calms, its fantastic creatures, its floating cemeteries—all have taken possession of his soul and have sharpened his eye until it has become a spearhead. There is something uncanny about the man. He suggests that vast and dim hinterland of our mind, in which are wont to generate the misgivings and vaticinations of conscience, where also from mood to mood flash those instincts of our immortality which like Northern Lights coruscate and are gone—a world lying outside the ordinary occasions of life and with which *our eating and drinking, marrying and giving in marriage* are too generally unconcerned. The mariner comes, as it were, panoplied with these interfusing adumbrations and radiances, and thrusts himself into the common flow of human life, arresting the gaiety of the hour, because it is laid upon him to tell his tale and speak its warning, and the wedding-guest is held, despite himself, until the tale is done

> The Mariner, whose eye is bright,
> Whose beard with age is hoar,
> Is gone ; and now the wedding-guest
> Turn'd from the bridegroom's door.
>
> He went like one that hath been stunn'd
> And is of sense forlorn ·
> A sadder and a wiser man
> He rose the morrow morn.

Just so Jonah comes from the sea to Nineveh. He comes as a foreigner with the strangeness of a far-off country in his accent. But more, the sea and its horrors still seem to cling to him. There is a wildness in his aspect. He is a scarred man, one who has been baptised in an experience of wild waters, a man who bears in his very eye a reminiscence of the hell from which he has so narrowly escaped. Clearly the hand of God is upon him. And the people of Nineveh cannot ignore him, nor shake him off. They are

THE BOOK AND THE SIGN

held by this ominous figure, thus arriving amidst their pleasures and traffic. He speaks nothing of himself, but in words full of awe and anger and utter fearlessness, he denounces the doom of the guilty city. Spell-bound beneath his preaching, the Ninevites, though notorious for hardness and cruelty, break down all about him, weeping like little children, and thus *repent at the preaching of Jonah*.

If in some such dramatic way the figure of Jonah moved through the spacious imagination of Jesus, though the tale were but a fiction it would have all the verisimilitude which a *Hamlet* or a *Macbeth* has to us, for its air and manner are native to that Eastern world in which Jesus lived. A recent writer and famous theologian, Professor Rudolf Otto, whose book, *The Idea of the Holy*, comes as a timely corrective to the placid religiosity of our time, has drawn an instructive picture of the Eastern holy man in the fascination he exerts over the minds of his fellows.

> The ' holy man ' or ' the prophet ' is from the outset, as regards the experience of the circle of his devotees, something more than ' a mere man ' ($\psi\iota\lambda\grave{o}s\ \check{a}\nu\theta\rho\omega\pi o s$). He is the being of wonder and mystery, who somehow or other is felt to belong to the higher order of things, to the side of the *numen*[1] itself. It is not that he himself teaches that he is such, but that he is experienced as such. (p. 162.)

Holy men, or prophets like these, the East, throughout its length and breadth, has often known. It was a perfectly natural mental movement in our Lord, therefore, which clothed Jonah with mystery, and conceived him as having been *a sign to the Ninevites*—a sign, in Professor Otto's language, of the Numen Itself—a sign of Him Who, both in the Old Testament and in the New, is *a consuming fire*, the sign of a God who from time to time with the flame of a sword cuts out the ulcerous centres from the body politic of our world.

---
[1] Prof. Otto uses this Latin word in the sense of a supernatural divine power which impresses our feeling but escapes both definition and ethical classification.

THE PROPHET JONAH

Even as Jonah became a sign unto the Ninevites, so shall also the Son of man be to this generation. The strange hold which Jesus has had upon the souls of men in all the centuries of our era began in those days when, despite all His grace and charm, men feared Him even while they were drawn to Him. *They were in the way, going up to Jerusalem; and they that followed were afraid.*[1] There was something transcendent about Him. He suggested another country than Israel's. He had his historic heritages but it seemed that for him, more than for any man, Earth was, in Wordsworth's phrase, only "a foster-mother." The fourth Gospel attributes to Him the statement, *Ye are from beneath; I am from above: ye are of this world; I am not of this world.*[2] One has always felt a little repelled by the bluntness of the words they do not savour much of His manner of speaking I believe they owe something to the evangelist's eagerness in battling for his Lord against the ingrained unbelief of a later time But substantially they are in accord with more authentic sayings of the Master reported by the Synoptists Far liker Him in form, and yet even more suggestive of His transcendence is that distinction He made in His parable of the husbandmen between the servants and the son—*He had yet one, a beloved son. he sent him last unto them, saying, They will reverence my son* [3] Or again, this transcendence meets us in the categories of the famous saying about His Return · *Of that day or that hour knoweth no one, not even the angels in heaven, neither the Son, but the Father* [4]

Upon Him too, as upon Jonah, lay the sense of the pressure of God His preaching was in words which were given Him to say. Here also the fourth Gospel is emphatic. *I spake not from myself; but the Father which sent me, he hath given me a commandment, what I should*

---

[1] S Mark x, 32
[2] S. John viii, 23
[3] S Mark xii, 1-12, and parallels.
[4] S. Mark xiii, 32.

THE BOOK AND THE SIGN

say, and what I should speak[1] And again too, less explicitly perhaps, but with the greater significance of parable, comes the word of Jesus in S. Luke, *I have a baptism to be baptized with; and how am I straitened till it be accomplished!*[2] There was a tremendous urgency in His message, especially as the end of His ministry drew near Ever deeper came the note of pleading, of warning and of anger. There had been a period about midway perhaps through His ministry, when the crowds fell off from Him, but at the end they could not shake themselves free. Indeed, then *the people all hung upon him, listening*[3] Yet what things He said! what rebukes! what scathes! what foreshadowings of doom! Echoes of Nineveh-preaching reverberate through His words True, the issue of His work was different from that of Jonah This, indeed, was His lament. But in His own soul He carried all those elements of personal greatness which, in the story of Jonah, are the only possible explanation of a whole nation's repentance—the bearing of a speaker who has found the high mission of God an unevadable command *This generation,* He said, *is an evil generation · it seeketh after a sign; and there shall no sign be given to it but the sign of Jonah For even as Jonah became a sign unto the Ninevites, so shall also the Son of man be to this generation* I fear this can only mean that for the generation to whom Jesus came His words of grace should wither into a dead letter, and only His language of doom be remembered, His profound sympathy with sinners be lost to view and only the awfulness of the Numen in Him be apparent If that is the meaning, unwelcome as naturally we find it, it is yet remarkable for its foreshadowing of the whole later history of Judaism in its relations with Christendom down to our own day. There have, of course, been many Jews who have followed Him. There is an increasing number of them who revere Him.

---

[1] *S John* xii, 49 There are many similar passages in this Gospel
[2] *S Luke* xii, 50
[3] *S Luke* xix, 48

But, broadly speaking, His significance with His own people has had no charm, no allurement of beauty. He has been only a messenger of the ill-will of God, a name associated with unspeakable calamities, and this for the most part without the justification of a moral dynamic working repentance in the doomed.

In his *Holy-Cross Day* Browning has presented a picture dealing with medieval times in Rome and the lot of the Jews therein It is a poem that humbles a Christian churchman to the dust, a mordant and searching bit of characteristic Browning-art. It makes one feel to the full the wickedness of our 'Christian' treatment of the Jew But the lines which chiefly make the poem memorable are those in which the despised Jew thinks upon Jesus:

> Thou ! if thou wast He, who at mid-watch came,
> By the starlight, naming a dubious name !
> And if, too heavy with sleep—too rash
> With fear—O Thou, if that martyr-gash
> Fell on Thee coming to take thine own,
> And we gave the Cross, when we owed the Throne—
>
> Thou art the Judge. We are bruised thus
> But, the Judgement over, join sides with us !
> Thine too is the cause ! and not more thine
> Than ours, is the work of these dogs and swine,
> Whose life laughs through and spits at their creed !
> Who maintain Thee in word, and defy Thee in deed !
>
> We withstood Christ then ? Be mindful how
> At least we withstand Barabbas now !
> Was our outrage sore ? But the worst we spared,
> To have called these—Christians, had we dared !
> Let defiance to them pay mistrust of Thee,
> And Rome make amends for Calvary !

That is not repentance, nor, as yet a saving faith in Him, but it betokens the beginning of a change towards better things, and after the manner of Browning's work generally, represents in reality more truly a modern than a medieval attitude The best Hebrew minds of to-day are not far removed from those of Christian leaders, and we are reminded of the saying of S Paul concerning his fellow-countrymen, *A veil lieth upon their heart, but whensoever a man shall turn to the Lord, the veil is taken away* [1]

It remains for us to realise that there is a message in this New Testament handling of the story of Jonah for the Christian Church as well as for Israel. I find in a recent biography an illustration of the Sign of Jonah as fulfilled in our Lord. Mr. Harold Begbie, in his *Life of William Booth, the Founder of the Salvation Army*, gives us the story of Booth's first London convert, an Irish prizefighter

" One morning," says this man, " I was walking towards the public house . . when I came across General Booth for the first time in my life . . . I looked at him. He looked at me. Something in the man's external appearance took hold of me then and there. I stopped dead in the street looking at him ; and he stopped, too, looking at me. . .   After he had looked at me a long while, says he very sadly, ' I'm looking for work.' I was taken aback. ' I've got no place,' says he, ' to put my head in ' I got hold of some coins in my pocket, and was just going to offer them to him, when he pointed to ' the boys ' outside the public house just opposite, a crowd of them, and says he, ' Look at those men,' he says, ' look at them ! —forgotten by God and man. Why should I be looking for work ? There's my work over there, looking for me But I've got no place,' he says, ' where I can put my head in.' ' You're right, sir,' I said ; ' those men are forgotten by God and man, and if you can do anything for them, 'twould be a great work ' And what made me say that ? Sure it was just the man's external appearance. He was the finest-looking gentleman ever you saw—white-faced, dark-eyed and a great black beard over his

[1] *II Corinthians* iii, 16

chest ; sure there was something strange about him that laid hold on a man."

Mr. Begbie adds, " I asked him to tell me whether the preacher did not say anything at that first interview which accounted in some measure for this instant effect upon his mind. But again and again he protested that it was ' just the man's external appearance,' hinting at some ghostly emanation, or psychic influence which laid a spell upon his senses." (Vol. I, pp. 366-8.)

This, though crudely described, was *the Sign of Jonah*. And as we turn the pages of the biography we see how that arresting ' external appearance,' the ' something strange ' in Booth was the outcome not so much of extraordinary talents as of a tremendous moral urgency, a deep sense of God's will driving the man into his life's work. He who has the *Sign of Jonah* is one who thus stands in the great succession of souls that have been baptised in *the heart of the seas* and thence have learnt the majesty of the laws of God, and the indissoluble responsibilities of every human being. And at all times in the history of the Kingdom of God here upon earth, there is little that can be done for human salvation that does not bear as its *imprimatur* this unmistakable token of God. And if with all this one knows, as Jesus knew, the *good pleasure of the Father*, and is baptised into the Spirit of Jesus, then something more yet is realised , the grace of the early Galilean preaching is recovered and by the quality of that moral temper which, despite all its indignation, grieved over the doom of Jerusalem with a sweeter grief than Jonah's grief over the lifting of Nineveh's doom, it may be said once more, *A greater than Jonah is here*

IX

THE SPIRIT OF CHRIST WHICH WAS IN THE AUTHOR

IX

THE SPIRIT OF CHRIST WHICH WAS IN THE AUTHOR

IF one had the ability, and the courage and the reverence to construct a discussion after the manner of Landor's famous *Imaginary Conversations*, between the Author of the *Book of Jonah* and Jesus Christ, it would surely open with some expression of surprise on the part of the Author at the way in which his book had been viewed by Jesus He should be made to point out that whereas the story had been written as a criticism of bigotry, Jesus had found in it a record of human greatness Our Lord would not answer the surprise of his interlocutor by any explanation. It would be left to the Author's second thinkings to realise that, if his story was to be taken seriously at all, whether a story of fact or of fiction, then so vast a conversion to repentance as that of the Ninevites, called for an adequate cause in the agency thus Divinely employed. But such an imaginary conversation should ere long deepen into a monologue of the Lord, as in the conversation between Him and Nicodemus, the silence of the Hebrew author covering a neophyte's joy in new unfoldings of truth. On His side, certainly, if actually they could have met, Jesus would have welcomed this old Hebrew writer as a man in whom His own spirit found large expression. Indeed, it is no profitless conjecture to say that since Moses and Elijah once were permitted to converse with Him touching the *decease he was about to accomplish at Jerusalem*, strengthening Him, doubtless by their insight into Death and Life, the Author of the *Book of Jonah* may have been similarly commissioned at some time to confirm Him in the wideness of His mercy towards all mankind. It remains for us to see the things in which the Spirit of Christ wrought in this man.

In the first place, the Author was certainly a patriot. If one can recognise a patriotic value in the prophet's blind hatred of those great world-powers at the hands of which Israel suffered so much, if something may be said at least to excuse his zeal for the destruction of Nineveh, there is a far nobler love of country manifest in our Author himself as he pourtrays the narrowness of all this for our emphatic reprobation. If in his work he pillories the Israel of his day, yet we must remember it is not always those who unqualifyingly panegyrize their nation who love it best Others who severely scourge its faults may love it more. One can feel certain that our Author was one who would not have troubled to write as he did had he not been solicitous for his country's welfare. There is a tenderness in his humour which reveals a heart in living sympathy with those whose faults he deplored We cannot fail to see this quality in the playfulness of Yahweh's treatment of Jonah. One pictures the figure of a stately man, such as those three Abraham saw at his tent door on the eve of the destruction of Sodom, some angel of Yahweh through whom the God deigned to speak, and one seems to see him stooping down and looking through the interstices of Jonah's faded, gourd-covered booth, and asking with an immense gravity, *Are you very angry?* There is no bitterness in the mockery, rather is it as the mild rebuke of a father's compassion for his sulking child. Indeed, that medieval paraphrase of *Jonah* which bears as its title *Patience*, and which has been referred to on a previous page, perhaps is not wholly outside the scope of legitimate interpretation in regarding the whole story as a narrative of the Divine discipline of a Hebrew believer through heritages of ancient enmity at work in his blood, mingled with trials that might daunt the bravest. In

THE BOOK AND THE SIGN 87

any case no one could write about his people as this man wrote without the inspiration of the love of country

In the second place, in the world of Revelation this book is the matrix of the doctrine of Internationalism   Most evidently the Author had that feeling of the value of other nations than his own out of which true internationalism must ever spring   He regarded all peoples as the work of God's hands   It is the Divine Artificer, workmanlike finding an interest in his own craft, who shapes the last question of the book, no longer a playful one but a question of the most concise and moving eloquence, *You have had a love for the gourd, which you have not laboured at nor made to grow. Child of a night it sprang up, and child of a night it perished   And I, should not I have pity upon Nineveh, the Great City, which has in it more than twelve times ten thousand persons who do not know how to distinguish their right hand from their left and also much cattle ?* These multitudes of the heathen—He had fashioned them, equipped them, wrought in their consciences, though they had developed so little according to His counsel and desire. Unable morally—so it seemed—to distinguish their right hand from their left, until some prophet should teach them, they might be adult in years but in character they were children—wilful, passionate, perishing without vision yet not without value   One is reminded here of what Dostoievsky wrote last century concerning his fellow countrymen ·   " The Russian masses ought not to be judged by the abominations which frequently they perpetrate, but by the many noble and radiant things which they produce amid their degradation."[1]   That is the liberal judgement of an ardent patriot.   The higher distinction of the Author of the *Book of Jonah* is that he exercises the same liberality in his envisagement of a foreign and hostile people, viewing them as undisciplined and overgrown children yet also as the work of God's hands   Such a spirit

[1] *Dostoievsky   his Life and Literary Activity*, by Eugenii Soloviev   English edition, p. 240.

as this is the generating atmosphere out of which the fellowship of all peoples at last will spring

Now both in its patriotism and in its internationalism the *Book of Jonah* exhibits characteristic workings of the Spirit of Christ He, too, condemned the Israel of His day, only because He felt in Himself the better soul of His people. Too little has been made of the patriotism of Jesus ; yet is it plain enough to any open-minded reader of the Gospels. He addresses Himself primarily, and bade His disciples do the same, to *the lost sheep of the house of Israel* (*S. Matthew* xv, 24, x, 5ff) The fourth Gospel is in fundamental agreement with the Synoptics, when it represents our Lord as identifying Himself with the pure Jewish race. *Ye worship that which ye know not. we worship that which we know for salvation is from the Jews* (*S. John* iv, 22). And, again, the same spirit that wept in Babylon, crying

> *If I forget thee, O Jerusalem,*
> *Let my right hand forget her cunning,*

broke into the impassioned lamentation of Jesus : *O Jerusalem, Jerusalem, which killeth the prophets, and stoneth them that are sent unto her ! how oft would I have gathered thy children together, even as a hen gathereth her chickens under her wings, and ye would not !* (*S Matthew* xxiii, 37).

But also our Lord's range of vision outwent the impulses of His contemporaries' patriotism. Passage after passage rises to one's mind, indicative of the vast sweep of His sympathies. Defiantly He throws the ægis of His name as a teacher over the boycotted Samaritan. In His forecasting of the Society He seeks to establish He declares, *They shall come from the east and the west, and from the north and the south, and shall sit down in the kingdom of God* (*S Luke* xiii, 29) ; and these are Gentiles !

It is not, however, merely in His recorded utterances that this wideness of His sympathy is made evident. There is that in His character which justifies His self-

THE BOOK AND THE SIGN 89

chosen title, *The Son of Man*, as a designation, which, whatever its origin, symbolises on His lips relationship with mankind as a whole. The appeal His personality has made, from the first century until now, to men of most widely divergent national types, reveals the working of a power which, if selective in its operation, has yet been broadly human too So it is that the Christian religion, generated long ages ago in that highest type of piety the *Book of Jonah* helped to produce, is designed to be the creator of the world's last International This it will shape, not in destruction of either classes or nations, but in the regeneration of our widely varied powers and sympathies.

Nationalism and Internationalism—these which both belong to the *Book of Jonah* and to the teaching and character of Jesus Christ claim a place in our final thoughts about this Scripture ; and in view of that oscillation between a base and indiscriminate glorying in one's country on the one hand and a morally unfruitful cosmopolitanism on the other, which so often marks the common mind of our time, some further consideration of these high themes may possess real value

Firstly, then, there is a patriotism—or nationalism, if the term be preferred—which is fundamental to personal character as the Bible seeks to establish it. It is no mere geographical affection ; it is more than an attachment to the particular land in which we happen to have been born. Whole peoples have sometimes migrated from one clime to another, and yet have clung together in a common affection. It is not based upon any foolish exaggeration of the greatness of one's own kindred Some of the smaller nations have exhibited this virtue in the most intense and ennobling form, free from all misconceptions as to their own relative importance in the world. Nor is it a consciousness of the superiority of the institutions, laws and customs of our country over those of our neighbours. Here, indeed, the critics of patriotism often shoot wide of the mark. Thus the French rationalist, Diderot, in the eighteenth century, declared, " By comparing among all nations laws with laws, talents with talents, and manners with manners, nations will find little reason to prefer themselves to others."[1] On the contrary a backward people, conscious of much barbarism often moves to a higher level of civilisation through the strength of national preference For the moral sanction of patriotism is this—where we have most received there our deepest obligation lies. I owe a debt of gratitude to my own nation deeper than I can ever owe elsewhere. Every one of us has received far more from his nation than he can ever contribute to it—heritages of language, of literature, of legal protection, and of an almost infinite mechanism for the operation of daily life. If at times other loyalties present claims that seem to conflict with national love, yet the way of duty opens for all men of honour when they bring to it the memory and measure of indebtedness

The problem of patriotism, however, is that of self-clarification. Love of country will have little value unless it express itself in moral discrimination between historic processes. The stream of life in our national history which has been noblest is that to which our loyalty is due. The unworthy elements of the past and of the present we are bound to repudiate. And the truth about our own loved British Isles is that, just as in Hebrew history, two streams of influence the narrowly national and the international are plainly discernible. On the one hand, it is probably true, as J. A. Froude once observed, that our Empire pioneers have been mostly men without much scruple or regard for other interests than those suggested by the flag. Whatever their private morals (and these not always quite correct), they have been little concerned with any idea of national altruism. They have fought and they have

---

[1] Morley's *Diderot*, 1, p 245. Morley seems to have approved the sentiment

THE BOOK AND THE SIGN

builded under no pretence of serving mankind. Indeed, towards other peoples they have often been pathetically contemptuous Sir F. H. Doyle's stirring poem, *The Private of the Buffs*, illustrates a typical English attitude. In the hands of a barbarous foe,

> Let dusky Indians whine and kneel;
> An English lad must die.

On the other hand, it is possible to trace in our history a current of nobler impulse slowly working towards political expression The late Professor J. A. Cramb, in his *Origin and Destiny of Imperial Britain*, observes:

> For this Empire (of Britain) is built upon a design more liberal even than that of Athens or the Rome of the Antonines. Britain conquers, but by the testimony of men of all races who have found refuge within her confines, she conquers less for herself than for humanity. 'The earth is man's' might be her watchword, and, as if she had caught the ocean's secret, her empire is the highway of nations That province, that territory, that State which is added to her sway, seems thereby redeemed for humanity rather than conquered for her own sons. (p. 96)

The struggle between these opposing tempers of national feeling is by no means ended yet. If the salvation of our country in every critical juncture of her history has been secured through her inherent righteousness—" The greatest Empire in the annals of Mankind," says Cramb[1] " is at once the most earnestly religious and the most tolerant "—yet it must be admitted our common Christianity is a very diluted thing We carry a tremendous persistence of Paganism in our blood, and, as a whole, the nation is not livingly interested in the rights of other peoples. And now we also, like Israel, have had our baptism in dreadful waters. What the Exile was to Israel the Great War has been to us. And the word of the Eternal has come to us a second time, recalling us to our trust—the moral leader-

[1] *op. cit.*, p. 78.

ship of mankind. For this, indeed, should be ours, partly through the geographical position and the facilities of the homeland we inhabit, partly through the fact that within the British Commonwealth of nations there is brought together a greater variety of peoples and languages than can be found within any other political bond. What response are we making to the Divine appeal ? For the quickening of our priestly vocation surely we have learnt something from the waves and billows that have passed over us with their nightmare of entangling seaweeds. Or have we, too, been plunged into the *belly of Hell* in vain ?

These are the questions which the *Book of Jonah* suggests for our people to-day They are questions which an unprejudiced survey of our present moral situation in domestic and in industrial life compels us to leave unanswered, even as in the brilliant Scripture we have been considering the dogged misanthropy of the Hebrew prophet is exhibited but not dissolved. And yet again, as in the *Book of Jonah* the last word is not with the prophet but with his God, so to us also a voice of the Spirit is still audible, pleading that we should build Jerusalem

In England's green and pleasant land

Surely, too, it has been the prompting of that same Spirit which has led to the framing of the Treaty of Locarno ; for whatever view may be taken of British commitments therein, some moral advance has been made beyond the old position of our friendship with France and Belgium in the pledge that British support henceforth will be accorded to whichever of the Western Powers may be the subject of aggression on those frontiers that lie nearest to us And we may well be hopeful of a statesmanship which plainly seeks to establish goodwill, not only between ourselves and our late allies, but in our relations with former foes as well.

I have somewhat anticipated what needs to be said as

THE BOOK AND THE SIGN 93

to the claims of Internationalism, for in truth we cannot serve the noblest factor in our national life without entertaining those claims. The world of duties is one, its hemispheres merge into one another. It needs to be asserted that there is no necessary conflict between nationalism and internationalism Rather, to borrow an illustration from a modern Jewish writer,[1] just as the earth revolves upon its own axis and yet moves round the sun, so a nation's actions may turn upon a centre of its own life, while also traversing an appointed path in the fellowship of the race

At the present time there is a very clamant need for the assertion and exposition of the Christian position. The Churches have been somewhat savagely and hypocritically scourged by people outside their ranks for sharing in the War-guilt of 1914. Whatever their sins have been, however much any renewed affirmation of the teaching of Christ may reflect upon their past, they must ever courageously assert the principles of reconciliation, forgiveness and goodwill between enemies But yet more urgently the doctrine of Christian Internationalism needs to be applied to racial questions. For in face of what has been truly called " the rising tide of colour against white world-supremacy " there are English and American writers whose attitude is frankly pagan Thus Mr. Madison Grant, in introducing Dr Stoddard's book on the Colour question, tells us the Anglo-Saxon must " shake off the shackles of an inveterate altruism, discard the vain phantom of Internationalism, and reassert the pride of race and the right of merit to rule." Our present condition, a very grave one, he holds, is largely " the result of following the leadership of idealists and philanthropic doctrinaires." And again, " Democratic ideals . . . in England or in America is one thing, but it is quite another for the white man to share his blood with, or entrust his ideals to brown, yellow, black, or red men. This is suicide pure and

[1] Prof Lazarus, *The Ethics of Judaism*, American edition, II, p. 226.

simple."[1] These are ominous sentences. The objection to mixed marriages is certainly not incompatible with a very wide inter-racial association. Even within the same nation, marriage out of one's own class is a fruitful cause of unhappiness, while yet we may all share together in political and religious ideals and in the endeavour to promote the welfare of our country. But the wholesale repudiation of idealistic leadership and the refusal to promote the white man's ideals outside his own territories, involves not only the repudiation of Christianity; it creates also the danger of that very race-suicide this American writer dreads; for in view of the admitted " rising tide of Colour " wars of the bitterest kind are almost certainly the alternative.

Here we must dare to reassert the comity of nations in the purpose of God. Whatever risks may seem to attend a more generous attitude to Colour than as yet has obtained, the ground of our confidence is the universalist belief which underlies the *Book of Jonah* and which emerges so plainly in the teaching of Christ. A recent work for which the whole Church may well be grateful, Mr J. H. Oldham's *Christianity and the Race Problem*, admirably exhibits the problems we have to face, emphasises the need for hard thinking towards practical solutions, and restates for us the Christian ideal. Yet is there something further to be said with full emphasis. Mr. Oldham rightly sees that the pressure of population is one of the most serious factors in international and inter-racial hostility. " The desire to obtain access to supplies of food and to the sources of wealth by which food may be purchased to meet the need of an expanding population is the chief cause of the national jealousies and rivalries by which the world is distracted to-day."[2] The facts and figures by which this aspect of the world-problem is shewn us may be all true enough, and the courageous plea for

[1] *The Rising Tide of Colour*, p xxxii.
[2] *Christianity and the Race Problem*, p. 205.

justice all round, whatever the resulting hardships to white peoples, is of the Christian faith. But it needs also to be said that our Faith is fixed upon the character of God. We are very inadequately equipped to measure the resources God has locked up in our world. Fifty years ago many people were seriously apprehensive that the coal measures of the world would ere long be exhausted and an Arctic prospect began to loom in the popular imagination. Now it appears to be difficult to find sufficient purchasers for our coal. The truth is, as Lord Balfour said in his Presidential Address to the British Association in 1904, " We seem to be practically concerned chiefly with the feebler forces of Nature, and with energy in its least powerful manifestations . . . We live, so to speak, merely on its fringe." Every day since these words were uttered has confirmed that view and opened up new hopes of Nature's resources for the supply of human needs. But whatever may be the range of scientific discoveries, if we know God as the Father of us all we have such sure confidence respecting the provision He has made for His world, as turns the appeal for the practice of inter-racial justice into a call for simple loyalty to ourselves. If it be said that this is a mere feeling and that we must face facts, the reply is that, to him who follows Christ, God is the Fact of facts.

To sum up · Not without foresight has the Sovereign Will brought upon their journey these vast and gifted peoples, whose ways so widely differ from those of the white man. Our insistence, therefore, is not only upon justice and truth in the white man's dealings with them, but also upon a believing good-will that they also, no less than ourselves, may be served, and themselves be encouraged to offer service, within the great Family of Mankind. Our publicists and statesmen often hesitate to deal generously in these matters because they see risks involved. Such apprehensions would fade before a real conviction as to the good pleasure of the Father. We plainly need more faith, and better. Then in all the intercourse of a Christian nation with other nations, coloured or white, policy would be directed along that line of ancient Hebrew thinking which asserted the priesthood of Israel as God's people among the various nations of the world. And this, the supreme contribution of the Old Testament, with which all the spiritual processes of the New agree, calls upon us to affirm that the noblest prerogative of a free and sovereign nation is the right to serve mankind.

NOTE C

THE LITERAL INTERPRETATION

NOTE C

THE LITERAL INTERPRETATION

A POPULAR statement of the conservative position in regard to the *Book of Jonah* has recently appeared entitled, *Jonah : Prophet and Patriot*, by D. E. Hart-Davies, M.A. In his endeavour to establish the historical character of the mission to Nineveh, the author quotes from the English version of *Tobit*. ' Tobit on his death-bed, addressing his son Tobias, gives him parting counsel in the words : " *Go into Media, my child, for I surely believe all the things which Jonah the prophet spake of Nineveh, that it shall be overthrown. . . . And now, my child, depart from Nineveh, because those things which the prophet Jonah spake shall surely come to pass.*" (xiv 3, 4, 8.)

Mr. Hart-Davies is apparently unaware that this translation is based upon MSS. which in Dr. Charles' standard work, *The Apocrypha and Pseudepigrapha of the Old Testament*, are regarded as of secondary value Unquestionably in place of *Jonah the Prophet* the true reading is that preserved in the famous *Sinaiticus* MS , *Nahum the Prophet*. A moment's reflection shews that this must be correct, because while the overthrow of Nineveh, in which Tobit so greatly rejoiced, accorded with the prophecy of Nahum, the prediction of Jonah was, as the *Book of Jonah* narrates, cancelled by the God who sent him

Also it must be said that Mr. Hart-Davies' method of quoting an imposing array of ancient authorities in favour of the historical character of Jonah's mission is really of very small value. It is no derogation from the greatness of these scholars to abandon their judgement upon a matter of this sort. I suppose an equally impressive catena could be made out in favour of the literal history of *Genesis* i, or, let us say, of the Ptolemaic astronomy. Such appeals are really irrelevant when once our modern standards and tests of literary criticism have approved themselves valid. Similarly it is of small use to exhibit the diversity of opinion amongst modern scholars concerning the details of the critical position. All that such a method really establishes is the mutual independence of such writers in their rejection of conservative theories. They cannot be said to confute one another, if, as Mr. Hart-Davies believes, they are all wrong.

But the most serious weakness in this writer's book is his endeavour to foreclose discussion by an appeal to the authority of Christ. Following *S. Matthew's* version of our Lord's reference to Jonah, and even declaring that *S. Luke's* has " no substantial difference from it " (p. 25), he repeatedly insists that this reference establishes the historicity of Jonah's adventure and mission. " The testimony of our Divine Lord," he affirms, " ought to be conclusive This has always been for me the insuperable objection to the allegorical interpretation of the narrative " (p. 24). He deals with various suggestions which have been made with a view to disencumbering the subject of Christ's words. Some of these suggestions have, certainly, been unfortunate but they make no appeal to most of those who adhere to the allegorical interpretation. We are not concerned here with any Kenotic theory of our Lord's person. All that need be said is that the question of the literary *genus* of the *Book of Jonah*, whether it should be treated as history or as allegory, was not raised in Christ's time, nor, as far as we can judge, was it before His mind at all. He had His own way of reading Scripture and did not always follow what appears to us to have been the original intention of the sacred writers An instance of this independence may be seen in His wonderfully illuminating quotation of *Exodus* iii, 6, *I am the God of Abraham,*

THE BOOK AND THE SIGN

and the God of Isaac, and the God of Jacob; to which **He** adds, *He is not the God of the dead, but of the living (S. Mark xii, 26-27).* There can be very little doubt that our Lord here reads into the words a meaning which their author never purposed, seeing that Moses is nowhere represented in the Pentateuch as believing in the life after death. That, while it in no way lessens the value of Christ's comment —for the great sayings of literature often contain more than their authors consciously realise—illustrates that independence of mind which is one of the most impressive features of His recorded words. Now, similarly, His treatment of the *Book of Jonah*, as I have been at some pains to shew in these studies, was quite apart from the author's intention, and this whether the book be classified as allegory or as history. I do not imagine, therefore, that even had the allegorical character of the book been clearly present in His thought it would have made any great difference to His use of the story. For, whether the men of Nineveh ever heard the preaching of a prophet called Jonah or not, we all know perfectly well what Jesus meant when He placed over against the type of people a repentant Nineveh would have exhibited the wilful and hypocritical amongst His own generation, against whom He was testifying. No one, either then or now, could imagine that He intended an actual standing together of the two bodies of people, thus compared, in some world-assembly, at a last great assize. His comparison held and holds good in its essential appeal whether Jonah's mission be fact or fiction. But the point cannot be too strongly insisted upon that the literary questions here involved were not in men's minds when He spoke, and it is a first-class mistake to invoke His authority outside that sphere of moral and religious truth with which alone He was concerned. He did not come to deal with literary criticism any more than He came to teach astronomy. In all those matters that are properly subject to scientific handling, He affected no omniscience. He was content to take over the stock of knowledge and opinion which He found commonly received by His fellow-men, and to make what use of these He could for those higher purposes which relate to sin and salvation.

www.ingramcontent.com/pod-product-compliance
Lightning Source LLC
Chambersburg PA
CBHW071145090426
42736CB00012B/2230